Cruci

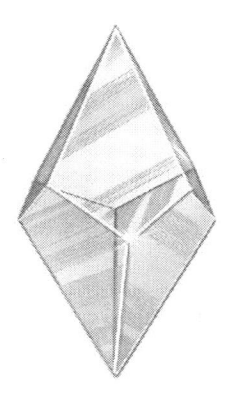

Crucible
Child Patriot American Victory

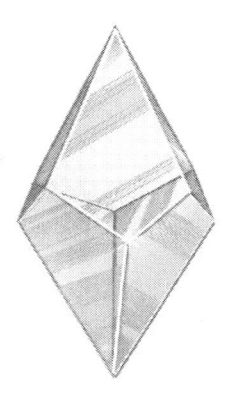

Köhne

Copyright © 2020 Jason Köhne

All rights reserved. Except for brief passages for critical articles or reviews, no portion of this book may be reproduced in any form or by any mechanical, electronic or other means, now known or hereafter invented, including photocopying, xerography, and recording, or in any information retrieval and storage system without the express written permission of the publisher.

Jason Köhne is also the author of *Born Guilty—Liable for Compensation Subject to Retaliation*, *Go Free—A Guide to Aligning with the Archetype of Westernkind*, *Prometheus Rising—Take Back Your Destiny*, and *It's a Comedy Dammit!*.

Jason Köhne (/ˈkuːnə/ *koo-nuh*)

Illustrated by Groundhog Fury

Printed by CreateSpace

NWG Productions

Dedication

I dedicate this work to white children. They will suffer far more than we have if we do not secure the Wellbeing of Westernkind.

Important Note: Friends, as I am a vocal champion for White Wellbeing, the antiwhites relentlessly endeavor to ruin me. I am not immune to these attacks. I need your help to stay afloat. Are you able to provide legal, financial, or some other assistance? Please reach out to me:

    Website: NoWhiteGuilt.org

    Collectibles: NoWhiteGuiltCollectibles.com

    LinkTree: https://linktr.ee/nowhiteguiltnwg

Thank you.

Contents

Crucible

1 Observance 1
2 Lost 4
3 The Door 6
4 A Wish 9
5 Heartbeat 12
6 Through the Door 17
7 Intolerance 21
8 Lesson in Respeck 25
9 Prophecy 29
10 Questioning the Faith 34
11 Heretic 39
12 Forsaken 42
13 Despair 46
14 Shunned 49
15 Collision Course 53
16 Alone 56
17 Inquisition 57
18 Talons 61
19 Persistence 66
20 Logic 69
21 Native 74
22 Death Threat 79
23 Righteous 82
24 Hunted 84
25 Blighted 88
26 A Club 90
27 Claws 94
28 Poisoned Faith 100
29 Imposters 102
30 Beyond the Walls 105
31 By Terror, They Rule 107
32 Heartache 110
33 Caught 114
34 Surrender 118
35 Darkness 123
36 Starlight 127
37 Preparation 130
38 New Rules 132
39 Identities 136
40 Targeted 138
41 Church Friend 140
42 Instigator 142
43 Must be Crazy 146
44 Pearls Before Swine 150
45 Blood of Deeds 161
46 Behind the Mask 164

47 Pretexts	169	56 Gathering Storm	217
48 Monster	172	57 Ancient Thunder	220
49 F in White Privilege	175	58 Damned Either Way	233
50 Honing	181	59 Clarity	237
51 Loyalties	187	60 Into the Monster's Den	240
52 Equal Treatment	192	61 The Spirit of the West	244
53 Turning Tide	201	62 Western Sunrise	258
54 Allies Within	204		
55 Counterstrike	209		

Appendix

Notate Bene	263	GO FREE	271

ALEA IACTA EST

VENI VIDI VICI

Chapter 1

Observance

I learned many things from my teachers and the media, but *his* was the name I heard more often than any other.

In the twilit classrooms of elementary school, the mechanical hum of rickety projectors lulled us into hypnosis, whirring and hissing, and billowing acrid clouds as the hymn and incense of liturgy, splashing his image across countless screens. Thirty-inch televisions, fed by VHS tape and infused with his countenance, bathed our upturned faces in flickering light—entrancing us with the celluloid deity and his zealous followers singing his praises.

Part man, part god, part saint, part savior—what more? I wasn't exactly sure, but I knew he was worshiped, that he was only spoken of and quoted in reverential tones, and that only in such tones were we permitted to speak of him.

Elementary school now behind me, a new era of my life had begun.

Day one in junior high school, and there I stood beneath a billboard, a shrine, a larger-than-life picture of this—man. Hanging ten feet above the floor, his was the only image in the communal area known as the Commons, where row upon row of lockers grew out of the carpeted floor, creating pews for the children who gathered there, the unwary disciples of the state's antiwhite religion, learning and worshiping under the fathomless stare of the state's new god: Martin Luther King, Jr.

Nailed to the floor before the Idol, I pondered the only name I had heard nearly as often as Martin Luther King, Jr. If this MLK represented all that was worthy of worship and adoration, the *other* represented his antithesis—the personification of unadulterated evil.

The former was said to be superior and savior: deliverer of unmatched wisdom, divinely inspired leader, intellectual visionary, persecuted martyr, and victim of white racism. The latter was said to be a murderer: slayer of millions of innocents, actuator of madness, and advocate of a demonic vision.

Chapter 1   *Observance*

In contrast to the black, saintly MLK, the demon's race was white, and his vision was informed by his concern for the wellbeing of the white race. If MLK is lord and savior, then Adolf Hitler—we were taught—is the devil.

It dawned on me that Christ and Lucifer had been replaced by MLK and Hitler. The doctrines, too, had changed: Where once we had Jesus Christ and the teachings of Christianity, we now had MLK and the teachings of antiwhitism—misleadingly named liberalism and progressivism by its deceitful advocates; and similarly, where we once had Lucifer's desperate effort to corrupt mankind and conquer the Christian Kingdom of Heaven, we now had Hitler and the desire to preserve the white race and Western Civilization.

Of course, other than what the Regime provided me, I knew nothing about Adolf Hitler. But I took offense at the assertion that the wellbeing of the white race equated to the genocide of nonwhites, because by linking nonwhite suffering with white dignity, the wellbeing of the white race became an evil. Moreover, by defining Hitler as the Beast, and then declaring that his chief concern was the survival of whites, the Regime (again) linked our wellbeing to matchless evil.

As an evil, its polar opposite makes a virtue of opposition toward white wellbeing—our dignity, identity, and inheritance. In other words, if concern for white wellbeing is immoral, then opposing white wellbeing is to fight immorality. It is to convince whites that it is virtuous to inflict harm on our people—evil to preserve it.

Chapter 2

Lost

I'm in the B's, but which way to the C's, a tremulous voice said in my head.

Trudging down a crowded hall, surrounded by students bumping each other as they studied their schedules while on the move, I vainly searched for my math class.

Elementary school had been nothing like this: Here, there were boyfriends who swaggered with arms around girlfriends, and girlfriends who slew rivals with glares to keep boyfriends, whites uniformed as *metal heads*, and nonwhites uniformed as *gangstas*, girls who wore too much makeup, and boys who could've used some makeup. There were kids with permanent scowls and others with unnatural smiles, boys who dressed shabbily and girls who dressed provocatively.

In essence, junior high school was a culture shock. I would need time to get my bearings.

Excuse me, I nervously attracted the attention of a teacher cheerfully strolling down the hall.

Embarrassedly holding up my class schedule, I asked, *Can you help me find my math class?*

Of course I can, she lilted, taking my schedule into her graceful hands.

Chapter 2   *Lost*

She had a beautiful face and kind, intelligent eyes. Dressed in a light blue-and-white dress that floated as she moved, and wearing a perfume that danced sweet notes through the air, she smiled brightly.

You want to keep heading this direction. It'll be on the right.

Thank...thank you, I mumbled, as she returned my schedule.

What's your name?

Jason Köhne, I answered, suddenly self-conscious of how I was standing and holding my arms.

Nice to meet you, Jason. I'm Mrs. Peyton.

She held out her hand and we shook. Her touch was as warm as her smile.

Bye now, she trilled, and she strolled away.

I'd like to get me some'a dat, hummed a black boy lustily as he followed Mrs. Peyton with his eyes and pinched at the crotch of his pants.

His friend, an orbicular white boy in a t-shirt too short for his sagging belly, laughed stupidly in wild fits as though he were choking.

Tell 'em to shut their mouths! a voice shouted in my head as heat rose up the back of my neck.

But then I noticed how much bigger they were, and my spirit lost its nerve like a dying wind drops a sail.

I stared at the floor and ignored their vulgar comments and laughter. I hated what they were doing, but the thought of confronting them was terrifying.

Chapter 3

The Door

Jason, come here and look at this, exclaimed Adam, an inquisitive but overly cautious friend of mine.

He was pointing at an open door off the Commons, beyond which curved a long, dark, narrow corridor. *Where do you think it goes?*

I don't know, I shrugged. *Let's find out.*

No! he gasped, grabbing a handful of the back of my shirt. *We could get in trouble.*

There's probably just a closet back there…or a utility room. We'll be fine.

Hold on, he protested, stalling. *We could…maybe we can ask—*

Hey what are you guys up to? interrupted Brian, a thin, blond boy who had been my best friend since 2nd grade. Decked out in his characteristic camo pants—Brian was a military buff—he and another friend named Chris (also occasionally known as Fearless for his, well, fearlessness) had ambled over.

Geeze, Chris, you could play for the NBA. You're more than a head taller than us, I remarked in surprise while silently noting his new, awkward gait.

Chapter 3 *The Door*

Standing next to Adam, who was a bit thicker and shorter than me and Brian, Chris looked like a great willow tree on the verge of losing its balance.

Though I had hung out with Adam and Brian throughout the summer, I hadn't seen Chris since the previous year.

How're y'all? Chris drawled.

Good—

I'm good—

How was your summer? I asked.

It was great. My family drove to Daytona for two weeks, Chris bragged, holding up two exuberant fingers.

You wouldn't believe the girls there! he added breathlessly, shaking his head with a look of disbelieving awe.

That's awesome, I jealously remarked.

Did you take pictures? chimed Adam, a bit too eagerly, turning red when we all looked at him.

Damn straight, I took pictures. I have like—thirty. I'll show you when you come over.

Still relishing the memory of his vacation, Chris grinned dreamily as I told him and Brian about the mysterious corridor.

We should check it out, I enthusiastically urged the group.

Both Brian's and Chris' faces lit with excitement, but Adam pleaded in a flurry, *No...look...we only have a few minutes to get to class.*

We can be late; it's the first week of school, argued Chris dismissively, adding, while squinting at his schedule under a confused wrinkle on his brow, *I don't even know where I have to go next....*

Adam nervously ran a hand through his dark hair as though hoping persuasive objections would pop out. When none did, he reluctantly nodded with a conceding, *Pfff.*

I patted him on the shoulder—*It'll be fine*—and then led the group toward the mysterious corridor, but as I neared the threshold, the bell sounded—we were late for class. When I turned back, I saw three conflicted faces.

What should we do? blurted Brian.

I'm going to class, said Adam.

Come on, objected Chris. *It'll only take a minute.*

See, Fearless is with me, I gibed, pointing at Chris and casting a mocking glance at Adam and Brian.

I don't care, retorted Adam testily. *I'm not going.*

Fine. Listen, I said placatingly to the group, *we'll go to class, but we have to agree that we're gonna find out what's down that hall—first chance we get. Agreed?*

Everyone nodded (Adam reluctantly) and we ran in different directions for our classes, casting curious glances over our shoulders at the dark doorway.

Chapter 4

A Wish

Quiet down. Quiet down, now. Um...Okay...okay everyone, said Mrs. Johnson, clapping her hands to get everyone's attention. *Let's get to know each other a little better. We'll start in this corner—* she pointed to her left—*and we will work around to the other side of the room. Each of you will tell the rest of us what you would wish for if you had only one wish—all right?*

A general flourish of excited whispers and giggles swept the room.

Greg and Ian, both friends of mine, turned to me with open-mouthed smiles.

I am so wishing to not be in school, joked Greg, his long silky hair (locks coveted by every girl in the school) framing his impish grin.

I'm wishing that tubby Tina over there would lose some weight, said Ian, his dark, perpetually sleepy eyes flashing with mock-malice.

We're starting with Abani, Mrs. Johnson said emphatically, silencing the room.

Go ahead, Abani. If you had one wish, what would it be?

Ummm, I'm not sure, mumbled Abani through her thick Indian accent, smiling awkwardly and casting quick, desperate glances at the girl sitting next to her.

Crucible

I felt bad for Abani: Everybody was staring at her, waiting for her to say something. Her mind had probably gone blank with embarrassment. I know mine would.

Mrs. Johnson cut in, helping Abani with her answer, which made me feel better. But I suddenly panicked: What was I going to say? What could I wish for? Something funny, to get a laugh? Or something serious, to make a point?

What about wanting the power to heal the sick? a speculative voice said in my head.

Since the birth of my brother, Gary, I had worried endlessly that he would succumb to his poor health. Gravely ill when he was born, he hadn't improved over the first two years of his life. I loved him fiercely, and I played and cuddled with him devotedly. I had even begged God to heal him, or to take my life rather than his.

It wasn't until I visited Gary at the therapy center that I realized how many other babies were ill. I had never felt so hopelessly saddened than when I saw those poor little boys and girls. *Why has this happened?* I had anxiously asked my mother, *Why aren't doctors able to do anything? Can't anybody help them?*

It was during one of those visits that I asked the Lord to give me the power to heal sick children. That was my one true wish, and I had kept it safely guarded in my heart.

Okay, Michael, what's your wish? Mrs. Johnson's Midwestern-accented voice startled me out of my contemplation.

Chapter 4 — *A Wish*

She was going through the class much faster than I had anticipated. Six kids had already given their answers and I hadn't heard one.

What am I gonna say? I urgently pressed myself. *I can't reveal my deepest wish. The boys'll laugh at me. They'll probably stop talking to me. What about wanting whites to show some pride in our heritage?*

I had always harbored an instinctual pride and allegiance to my people. I had always been saddened by the lack of self-respect I saw in whites, especially because so many of my nonwhite friends had such firm identities and ardent pride in their peoples.

Li, you're next, said Mrs. Johnson coaxingly, still moving quickly through the room.

But I don't know, I continued in my head. *Wishing my people would show some pride in our heritage is heavy. What'll everyone think? What'll they say? That I'm taking this game too seriously—probably. They'll probably laugh at me, too. No. It's too serious of a wish. I have to think of something else....*

Jason, said Mrs. Johnson, the whole class turning expectantly toward me. *What's your wish?*

That this game was over, I said with an upturn, as though it was a hopeful question. A few kids laughed. It was as good as I could've hoped for; at least my answer hadn't cost me any friends.

Chapter 5

Heartbeat

Heather pitched the kickball—no bounce or spin.

I ran forward and kicked it skyward. It soared toward the outfield, past the two kids gawking from second base, over the heads of the four scrambling kids in right-center field, and it was still sailing through the air when I glanced at it after rounding first base.

My knees churned beneath me, my feet spraying rocks and dirt as I ran. Second base flashed by. I banked my right foot off third a moment later, and then I slowed to a jog: The outfielders had only just reached the ball.

My team cheered and shook the fence as I crossed home plate.

Still breathing heavy, I slapped high and low fives with my teammates as I returned to the dugout. Finding Brian in high spirits, he and I grabbed a spot on the bench.

On days like today, roofed by a bright, warm sun and a deep, blue sky, our gym teachers led us outside for games of soccer, field hockey, and kickball.

You flew around the diamond! Brian exclaimed, gaping at me with an astounded smile.

Yeah but did Fox see me? I panted, nodding in the direction of Ashley Fox, one of the three hottest girls in the school, collectively and reverentially known amongst the boys as "The Triad."

Yeah, she did! She was cheering, too.

Chapter 5 — Heartbeat

Really?! Are you serious?!

My eyes went wide, my heart took to the air, a big band began to play and fireworks whizzed and popped kaleidoscopically.

Yeah. And she was smiling at you when you came home. Didn't you see her?

No! Damn! I didn't.

I looked hopefully over at Fox, standing behind the backstop and talking to one of her friends. *Man,* I dreamily mused, *I would give anything to see her smile at me.*

She was my first crush. Friendly, beautiful, and lighthearted, her face smiled even when she wasn't smiling. Just seeing her made me feel nervous and happy. The truth was that I hoped more than anything in the world to get her to notice and like me before the end of the year.

Way to kick the ball, Jason, said Kevin, as he and Mark sat down beside us, both of whom were good friends of mine.

Kevin had the quintessential look of a surfer, and consequently always made me think of and (odd as it may seem) smell the beach. Mark, on the other hand, was built like a tank; thick limbs and a barrel chest, and was the only kid I knew who was already starting a beard.

If I were as fast as you, I'd try out for the Bears, rumbled Mark wistfully.

Yeah? Well, if I were as strong as you, I'd wrestle bears for the circus, I retorted.

We laughed, but Kevin stopped us short with a look of keen interest.

Hey! He leaned in and lowered his voice. *I heard you dudes know where there's a secret passage.*

Yeah, I answered, *but it's not a secret. We just don't know where it goes. And the door's been shut every time I've seen it since.*

Is it locked? asked Mark, sidling in a little closer.

I don't know—maybe.

Suddenly lighting up, Brian said, *I meant to tell you that Adam told me he asked an 8th grader about it.*

What did he say? Mark and I nearly chorused.

Brian peered suspiciously at the other kids in the dugout. *Let's get out of here and I'll tell you.*

We followed him a few yards away from the field and then huddled like football players in a blizzard.

Somber-faced, Brian held each of our eyes before starting.

Adam said the 8th grader told him that nobody knows for sure what's at the end of that hallway, but that one kid had heard some of the teachers talking about it like it was a secret room or something.

A secret room for what? I asked doubtfully.

The teachers already have a lounge. I know where it's at, said Kevin easily, unimpressed by the revelation.

Nooo, Brian continued darkly. *It's supposed to be a place where they talk about serious stuff. And they say students are never taken in there except for expulsions.*

Chapter 5 *Heartbeat*

Sounds like you'll get in some deep shit if you get caught in there, puffed Mark, unconsciously flexing and rubbing his bulbous bicep.

I still want to see it for myself, I said, undaunted.

Well, yeah—me too, said Brian with a bit of worry swimming in his features. *I'm just nervous.*

Dude! Jason! When you dudes get expelled, you can tell me what you found, warned Kevin, casting a curious eye over the soccer field at three men who were busily talking and pointing across the school's back lot.

Who are they? I asked Kevin, concerned by their grim demeanor.

The black dude is Vice Principle Cribbs. He acts like he's cool, but he can be a real hard ass. The guy with the sheep's hair is Mr. Wolf. He's a guidance director. He's pretty laid back, but he doesn't mess around.

Who's the other guy with the glasses? I pressed.

That dude is Principal Stein. Nobody knows what he's like because if you're sent to him—you're getting kicked out of school. He leaned in closer for effect, exaggeratedly forming his lips around the word: *Expelled.*

Hey! Kevin continued, leaping back in mock discovery, *maybe he expels you in that secret room....*

How do you know Stein expels everyone he sees? shot Mark incredulously.

My brother went here for two years, dude. Remember?

Crucible

Oh yeah. Sorry, offered Mark, shaking his head while massaging his other bicep.

They're leaving, noticed Brian with a sigh of relief.

You dudes'll be seeing Principal Stein soon enough, Kevin assured, as though our end was near.

Chapter 6

Through the Door

The door's open, I blurted excitedly to Brian, panting from the scamper to his locker.

It was the first time the door had been open in days. I had begun to think we would never know the truth about what lay at the end of the dark and intimidating corridor.

Really?! he exclaimed with a start, feigning excitement while glancing apprehensively in the corridor's direction.

It seemed the ominous stories had worried him more than he let on.

We're heading in after this period—It'll be fine, I added in a reassuring tone as worry tugged at his brow. *Make sure you tell Adam. I'll tell Chris.*

Minutes later, I hustled up beside Chris on my way to English.

That hallway's open, I whispered up at him as though I were a ventriloquist, not wanting to attract undue attention.

His eyes fleetingly sparked with excitement, but there was also a mote of trepidation. I guess even Fearless himself had been shaken by the grim tales of punishment.

Honestly, I was worried, too. But the stories seemed illogical. They didn't have the ring of truth. They felt like yarns older kids spin to frighten their juniors—or to hide something we would want or ought to know.

We're heading over after this period.

Cool, he breathed, grinning mischievously as his confidence returned. *I'll see y'all there.*

I was warmly surprised to see Adam waiting for me outside the dark corridor after class, fidgeting though he was with the zipper on his bag and looking profoundly guilty. He had been the most reluctant to explore the corridor. But then again, he had a streak of resilient loyalty that crept beneath his fervent cautiousness.

If I don't have a heart attack, he groaned heavily, running his hand briskly through his hair and gazing around as though looking for a firing squad.

Adam, you're 12—you're not gonna have a heart attack.

Hastening from one class to the next, students scuttled into the Commons, raucously packing it to the point of bursting. Though nearly surrounded, no one paid any attention to us as we impatiently waited for Brian and Chris.

There they are, Adam said in a disappointed voice, revealing a tenuous hope that the adventure would be scuttled in their absence.

Is everybody ready? I asked encouragingly, hopeful I wouldn't have to leave anyone behind.

They nodded as though gravely resigning themselves to a one-way trip.

Brian by my side, I nervously led the group through the open door.

Chapter 6 — *Through the Door*

As we crept down the narrow corridor, the florescent light and clamor from the Commons unnaturally faded behind us with the hall's curvature, leaving us in almost total darkness and silence.

Cocooned by a raven hush, a tremble worked through my hands. Our shallow, labored breath bounced off the cool stone walls, and dread beckoned us from the shadows ahead.

Let's go back. There's nothing in here, furiously hissed Adam's voice from somewhere in the darkness behind me.

No, wait—I can see light, I whispered back as a faint golden hue slithered enticingly along the corridor's arched ceiling and graceful bend.

Suddenly, the walls and ceiling flew away in all directions, and we were standing in a dimly lit auditorium. To my right, wide seats soared toward a distant ceiling, and to my left a polished black stage spilled like a half-moon oil-slick into the room, nearly as deep as I was tall.

We gazed speechlessly at the cavernous room: empty, silent, and eerily lit by no more than a few stage lights.

After climbing into the third row of seats, I turned around to face the others.

Amplified by some property of the room, Adam's hasty whisper sounded like squealing tires in the silence. *Come on. Let's go!*

He was hurriedly motioning for us to follow him as he backed uncertainly toward the dark hall.

I looked up at the gleaming stage. Soaring crimson curtains draped like velvet waterfalls spilling to the floor. The scent of scorched dust wafted from hot lamps in fitful shards across the stage and over the seats.

I could be an actor, I mused hopefully.

A mirage played into my mind's eye, a vision of myself on the stage, performing before a spellbound audience. *Yes...an actor...but I love science and history, and what about football and baseball?* I pondered, feeling that nothing in the world could stand between me and my dreams.

May I ask what you boys are doing? said a man's voice smoothly from the darkness at the back of the stage.

I shook from my reverie. Adam, Brian, and Chris whipped their heads toward the question, and then froze at the sound of approaching footfalls on the stage's polished floor.

As though gathering from the ether, a tall, slender man glided from the darkness. Handsome, brown haired and sporting a thick mustache, he eyed each of us suspiciously.

We were just looking, Brian confessed nervously.

The man, a teacher by the name of Mr. Albright, eyed his wristwatch appraisingly. *You have less than a minute to get to your next class. I suggest you hurry.*

Like field mice from the night-shadow of an airborne owl, we scrambled for the exit.

Chapter 7

Intolerance

On the contrary, I'm glad he was fired, Samantha. Racists have no place in our society.

*Of course, Joan—of course, I agree with you—*Samantha placed her hands on the desk, steadying herself—*but I feel he should have been reprimanded rather than fired. It was only a comment.*

Joan fixed Samantha with a scathing glare.

*Only a comment? Any comment that undermines a righting of historical wrongs is much more than a comment. It's…it's—*she self-righteously straightened herself to her maximum height—*It's a crime!*

Ms. Joan Brown, an 8th grade teacher, was getting heated in her conversation with Mrs. Samantha Swan at the library's checkout desk. When they started talking, we couldn't hear what they were saying, but as things became increasingly animated, we heard every word from our seats in the center of the library.

Jason, man, you think they're gonna fight? droned Ian lethargically, an eager grin spreading under his sleepy eyes.

What? No. Be quiet for a minute so we can listen, I said, knowing we only had seconds before the start of class.

Joan, I heard he can't get a job because of this. For God's sake, he has a family—two toddlers and a teen, continued Mrs. Swan in a pleading, defeated way, pressing one hand flat to her chest.

That's his problem, breathed Ms. Brown icily through razor-thin lips.

The bell rang and we turned to face our teacher, Mrs. Thomas, who was standing in front of the class in a pantsuit that made her look like a frumpy conductor.

Class—Mrs. Swan will be joining us today. She gestured in Mrs. Swan's direction as she bustled over. *She's a teacher's aide, and I expect you to give her the same respect you give me.*

We're meeting in the library today because you are going to spend the period researching the topics you chose for your book reports. Mrs. Swan and I will be available to help you with your projects. Now hop to it, she ordered, snapping her fingers.

There was a muted bustle as the class fanned out, some heading toward the catalog computers and others heading for the shelves.

Who do you think would win? asked Ian's monotone voice from over my right shoulder, as I ran a finger along the spines of plastic-jacketed books on a shelf.

Who would win what? I answered without turning around.

A fight—between the short lady and the mean one.

Ian, I spun around, *what kind of question is that?*

He didn't respond; he just smiled with his half-closed eyes.

The mean one, I said flatly, turning back to my work. *She's cold and vicious as all hell.*

Ha ha, I knew it, he shouted, pointing at the side of my face as though he'd won a bet.

Chapter 7 *Intolerance*

Be quiet! hissed a horrified librarian, scowling at us from two rows over.

We smiled guiltily.

Sorry—

I'm sorry—

I knew it, he continued, whispering in comic tones. *Me, too. That mean one was a snapping turtle.*

A snapping turtle?

Yeah, ugly and snappy.

Movement at the end of the row caught my eye. Mrs. Swan had turned the corner with one of the painfully shy girls from class, patting her reassuringly on the back.

It's okay, honey. I'll stay with you until we find all the books you need.

Excuse us, I said, nodding respectfully as we passed them on our way to the next row.

Fifteen minutes later, I was sitting at my table with a small stack of books when Mrs. Swan sat down across from me.

Mrs. Thomas told me you're Jason, she said with a warm, caring smile.

I looked up from my reading. *Hi.*

A sweet woman with a simple charm and a motherly demeanor, Mrs. Swan wielded a magic that made everyone happy—with the exception of Ms. Brown, of course.

Casting an impressed glance at the pile of books I had assembled, she asked, *How's your research coming? Looks like you're ahead of everyone else.*

I just want to do well. This is all new—a new school and all. Junior high school—it's a little scary...it seems like a big step.

It is a big step, sugar. And that's a great attitude. Have you made any plans for this year?

Oh yeah. I'm gonna concentrate on my school work and get good grades—make friends, and I want to learn about all the neat subjects taught here. Elementary school was nothing like this.

That's wonderful! she beamed. *I'm going to keep my eye on you, Jason—I know you'll go far.*

Chapter 8

Lesson in Respeck

I was wrenching my history book from my jam-packed locker when Greg and Chris walked up wearing curious grins.

What's up, boss, began Chris pregnantly, as though he had something intensely interesting on his mind.

Nothing. Just getting ready to go to history.

Heard about your two touchdowns on Saturday—Ken was talking about it last period—said if it wasn't for you, you guys would've lost. His smile—puzzlingly—bared too many teeth for the subject.

Did he? Well, if it wasn't for his blocking, I couldn't have gotten any yards—much less touchdowns, I finished, leaning into my locker door, forcing it shut like an over-packed suitcase.

Playing youth football had its benefits, not the least of which was public acclaim.

Yeah, but that's not the half of it, said Greg, leaning against a locker and folding his arms knowingly. *Fox heard the whole conversation. She asked if you had a girlfriend.*

What?! No way! I said disbelievingly.

She did, added Chris in a serious tone.

What else did she say?!

That's it, man—began Chris before Greg cut in.

No—she asked Ken what position Jason played.

Oh yeah, that's right, Chris nodded thoughtfully.

Every ounce of my spirit wanted to know more about Fox's question (like if it had seemed offhanded or interested, how she was standing or sitting, if she had smiled and a number of other minutiae that Chris and Greg had no way of knowing), but a black boy's angry shouts startled us out of conversation—and me out of bliss: *I'm not playen, motha-fucka!*

Greg, Chris, and I hurried over to where a jostling crowd had gathered. We pushed our way in as the shouting continued: *Dis motha-fucka think he gonna—*

Fuck'em up, stridently bellowed a black girl with a voice like a barbed whip, shoving her way through the crowd, large curls glistening on the top of her head.

He gotta learn respeck, roared another black boy, whom I saw over the heads of kids in front of me. His hands held out to his sides, he marched and swayed menacingly as he brought his right fist into his left palm with an intimidating—POP!

As we pushed through the inner ring of onlookers, I saw a couple of black kids gesturing and jabbering threateningly near a large black boy who had a small white boy pinned against the cinderblock wall.

The black boy had a fistful of the kid's shirt, pressing it heavily into his throat.

If you scuffed my BK's I'ma fuck you up, motha-fucka, growled the black boy, wetting his thick lips with a wild tongue and drawing back his free hand into a fist.

Chapter 8 *Lesson in Respeck*

Pure terror contorted the white boy's face: His neck was bright red from the pressure of the large black fist, and his hands were pressed flat against the wall in a gesture of total submission.

What's going on? I asked absentmindedly, seeing but hardly comprehending.

The white kid got in the big kid's way and they walked into each other—scuffed his BK's I think, said a boy's excited voice to my right.

BK was short for British Knights, which were flamboyant sneakers that black kids coveted.

Still pinning the white kid to the wall, the black boy slipped off his shoe and examined it: They rarely tied their BKs; rather, they left them loose, putting small knots at the ends of the laces.

You're lucky, bitch! said the black boy, satisfied that his sneakers hadn't been scuffed. Then, like he was punishing a dog, he slapped the white kid in the face with the bottom of his shoe.

A sharp scream escaped the white boy's tight lips, and then the black kid released him to the feral laughter of several blacks.

You gotta respeck, motha-fucka, said the black boy as he slipped his shoe back on, stomping it against the floor until his heel sank into it. *Get out the way next time!*

I was in shock. I had never seen anyone behave so cruelly. I had never seen anyone so terrified. And I suddenly realized that I hated myself for not intervening. I hated myself for being so afraid of being in a fight that I did nothing.

Crucible

Kids scrambled as they made a wide path for the sauntering thugs, who were cackling and already mirthfully recounting the terror on the white kid's face.

As the crowd thinned and the din of conversation grew, a white boy's voice cut though the chatter, *You don't mess with the blacks....*

It wasn't just the black kids, though. Despite being the majority, white kids feared most nonwhites, and they had ample reason to be afraid: Nonwhites often terrorized them, ganging up on and beating them up with impunity—even as crowds of whites looked on.

I glanced back at the little white kid as he picked up his bookbag and hustled off, his face red, his mouth frowning, and silent tears streaming down his cheeks.

Chapter 9

Prophecy

The teachers, the textbooks, and the movies at my junior high school spoke endlessly about "equality," about "inclusion," about "tolerance." But curiously—unless we showed hostility toward our fellow whites—my people were always excluded from these principles.

Nonwhite cultures and peoples were celebrated, while my people (when not antiwhite) were always cast as bad guys: as thieves, exploiters, destroyers. Such antiwhite rhetoric was so common I could recall its influential presence as far back as my earliest memories, but here the intensity was heightened, the enumeration of our "evils" lengthier, the justifications for retaliation against us more numerous—even if no more logical.

The narrative was clearly antiwhite. My only question was whether or not it was intentional or accidental—malice aforethought or an unintended consequence of some other objective. Everything pointed to intentionality, but I couldn't wrap my head around that possibility.

To be intentional meant that my people had been purposefully compromised, convinced not to defend themselves. It meant that people were claiming to do good when they knew they were doing evil. It meant that there was a power far greater and wealthier than I could imagine, a power relentlessly pushing for this narrative from deep within the workings of society.

You killed the mood, Jason. Why do you always bring this stuff up? whined Kevin as we lazed on our bikes near the school's front doors one Sunday afternoon.

Because it's important. We need to know whether or not they are against us on purpose, I retorted as the group glanced at a passenger airplane descending on Dulles.

I think they are! I hadn't thought about it like that until I started hanging out with you. But I asked my dad and he thinks so, too, shot Chris emphatically, looking far too tall for his neon-green Mongoose bicycle.

Adam, Brian, Greg, Ian, Kevin, Mark and I looked over at Chris, his passion surprising us.

I hate how we're always the bad guys, he continued. *It's like every freaking time I turn around my teacher or the TV is saying, 'evil white guy'—'evil white country'—'evil white boss'—'evil white leader.'*

I looked at the others and saw agreement and pain on their faces. And I saw that—being powerless—they had surrendered to the Antiwhite Narrative.

My dad told me not to say anything. He said I'd get kicked out of school. Imitating his father's deep voice, Chris continued. *'Keep your head down and just get through it, Chris,' he told me.*

Chapter 9 *Prophecy*

My dad said the same thing, dude, said Kevin in a hopeless sort of voice. *It's like this country hates us or something (You got that right!* added Brian)—*like it wants us gone, or dead.*

But is it on purpose? I mean, if we say something about it, maybe we—

You better not say anything, Jason, interrupted Greg gloomily from under his long hair, leaning over his handlebars and picking a rock from the tread on his tire. *My mom and dad get all weird about it when I've asked—like they're scared.*

What'd you ask them? said Mark, pulling down the brim of his Giants baseball cap to shield his eyes from the Sun's brilliant reflection on the school's windows.

Same thing that Chris is talking about—why we're always portrayed as the bad guys in history and TV—and movies.

I know! I hate that shit, spat Ian in an angry tone, his sleepy eyes wider than I had ever seen them. *We're the bad guys in every show I watch.*

I'm tellen y'all—this country hates us from the president on down to our teachers, vented Chris, dispiritedly gazing into the asphalt. *Just look at history class; the whole class is about how awful we are.*

Yeah. We're only the good guys when we're killing white people, added Mark sourly.

Brian pulled a compass out of his camo-pants and popped it open, examining its spinning metal face. *The blacks and Mexicans push us around all the time, calling us 'white mother-fucker' and shit like that—and no one ever says they're racist. My brother's friend was jumped last year by two black kids who beat the crap out of him. He had stitches on his face—his face! No one said they were racists. But if two white kids ever jump a black kid—man...they'll be burned at the stake.*

Aside from Ian and myself, everyone averted eye contact when talking about the issue as though ashamed or afraid to mention the double standard, or to complain about the treatment we were ceaselessly told we richly deserved.

I think I might mention it to the teachers—just ask them, you know. What could it hurt?

Don't do it, Jason, darkly warned Adam. *You go around asking questions like that and there's no telling. You ask questions like that and you won't have to worry about blacks and Mexicans kicking the crap out of you, because the whole system'll come after you!*

*Jason—*started Kevin.

No—hold on, Adam cut him off. *You've shown us a hundred times how the system singles us out as bad, right? Man, you start talking about that stuff and they'll—they'll set a monster loose on your ass* (*Yup,* added Greg pointedly).

Something about the word *monster* leapt out at me, swelling it beyond the other words in Adam's sentence, striking me deeper than it should have—almost forebodingly.

No monster or whatever is gonna come after me, I said to reassure myself and the group. *I'm just gonna mention it to the teachers. They won't care—no worries.*

Chapter 9   *Prophecy*

I don't know, Jason. Dude, you know they're not gonna take it well, said Kevin, looking anxious.

Kevin's right, bolstered Adam flatly. *You'll just get in trouble.*

I'm just gonna point it out, that's all. Maybe ask 'em why. You know, why can't we be proud, too—sort of thing. Why are we always the bad guys? See what they say....

Chapter 10

Questioning the Faith

I know you're not Hitler, one of my teachers impatiently condescended with a silencing wave of her hand, echoing and foreshadowing similar statements by most of my teachers. *But we all know where those questions lead—don't we? We all know those questions lead to the oppression of minorities…to Nazism and the Ku Klux Klan.*

I had asked why it was wrong for whites to be proud of our people. My questions were met with farfetched invocations of Adolf Hitler and the implication that I was just like him—*he asked such questions, he cared about the white race.*

I began to wonder if Hitler's concern for whites, or his crimes, or both, had been exaggerated, but I had no desire to explore the subject. I was preoccupied with my school work, sports, and researching the lives of my newfound heroes: Men—I would soon discover—the Regime deemed "demonic" as well, though of a lower "demonic order" than Hitler.

Men like Robert E. Lee, Stonewall Jackson, and the Grey Ghost, John Singleton Mosby stirred my imagination and evoked my admiration. I esteemed the unbiased information I gathered on them: their courage in waging a defensive war against an implacable enemy and insurmountable odds, their inventiveness, cunning, and artifice. I felt that they—and other Western champions I discovered on my

Chapter 10 *Questioning the Faith*

own—exhibited behaviors that epitomized the warrior ethos, an ethos I revered as vastly superior to antiwhitism and the African, hip-hop American culture.

More importantly, I instinctively felt a connection to them. I felt that they were *my* kin, *my* nation, that their spirit was *my* spirit, and that I too could do great deeds for my people. In the model of these noble warriors, and spurred by my confusion over the motivations behind the Regime's antiwhite rhetoric, I continued pressing my teachers for answers, but I also turned to my white peers for their opinions: We were the people condemned to pay an eternal compensation, to suffer an eternal guilt and "justified" retaliation. Surely they would rise to their own defense.

As I engaged others, I began to appreciate the role played by MLK in the Antiwhite Narrative. He was the immaculate god of this new religion, and we, the white race, were the demons whose evil deeds had brought him forth to deliver the innocent, demons—no matter our age or opinions—who had personally nailed him to the cross.

Is this the narrative by which we desire to live? I wondered. Does it serve our interests? Is it good for us to be consigned to such a role, to an eternal rejection of our identity, an eternal punishment based on our birth? Is it good for us to reject our right to self-interest so that we might receive grace from the antiwhite priests of the Regime's religion?

With these questions in mind, I turned my attention to our new "god." I queried my teachers and classmates about the shrine to MLK.

Crucible

I also argued that a larger-than-life portrait of a fellow Virginian, such as Robert E. Lee or Thomas Jefferson, should also grace the Commons.

Why Martin Luther King?

He was a champion of his people, my teachers proudly declared, breathless with obligatory homage. *He fought for their rights—he fought for the rights of all minorities. He fought against the racists—against bigotry, cowardice, and intolerance. He stood for equality, justice, and a righting of historical wrongs—the racial injustices of the past. He embodies the continued struggle against racism and inequality. He's a hero.*

You mean white people when you say "racists," right? I inconveniently asked repeatedly, putting my teachers on the spot, already knowing the answer. *I mean, when you're talking about nonwhites around the world fighting for freedom against the racists, you're not talking about nonwhites fighting against other groups of nonwhites, right?*

Anyone can be racist, but yes…when we talk about racists, we're talking about white racism, they unashamedly affirmed, nodding in the hope that I would unquestioningly adopt their antiwhite faith.

Some went so far as to define racism as a uniquely white phenomenon.

Racism is an element of European colonialism and exploitation, they sermonized, puffed-up with affected refinement, *so*

Chapter 10   Questioning the Faith

when minorities oppose other minorities, it's because of economic or territorial disputes—issues like that.

Whites don't wage war against nonwhites for economic and territorial reasons?

Well they do...but they're also motivated by racism...it's different...understand?

When I thought about what they were saying—stripped of the deception and noble sounding pretexts—I was infuriated.

Since they meant "white" when they said "racial injustice," "intolerance," "racist," "bigotry" and the rest, all I had to do was replace those words with "white" to decode what they were actually saying:

(*MLK was a champion of his people. He fought for their rights—he fought for the rights of all nonwhite peoples. He fought against white people—against the bigotry of whites, the cowardice of whites, and the intolerance of whites. He stood for equality, justice, and a righting of historical wrongs—the white-engineered racial injustices of the past. He embodies the continued struggle against white people.... He's a hero.*)

Undeterred, I lobbied my teachers to have portraits or busts of Lee or Jefferson added to the Commons—*Why not them?*

Squinting suspiciously, they threw appraising glances at me as though probing for signs of the Devil.

They owned slaves, they gravely affirmed, as though my question was shockingly stupid. *Jefferson probably raped his slaves, and Lee fought to keep black Americans oppressed and in bondage.*

Though they both may have had some admirable qualities, they were wicked men. They represent a social structure that has oppressed and exploited people of color for thousands of years. They represent everything we oppose. That's why they won't be displayed in the Commons.

But they're heroes of my people…and they were Virginians! I adamantly protested, wide-eyed with disbelief.

Nelson Mandela, a man of "peace" and "equality," they zealously assured me, *will hang in the Commons before either of them.*

Chapter 11

Heretic

Like quicksilver, the word spread throughout the student body that a "sevie" (the derogatory name applied to 7th graders) had asked that a portrait of Lee or Jefferson hang in the Commons: A thousand students in attendance at my junior high school, and they had nothing better to talk about.

Dude, you might as well give up. The teachers obviously don't care, and you know you're eventually gonna get it, advised Kevin as we passed in the hall one day.

Adam's warning, however, was much more ominous: *Everybody's talking about you. It's gettin' serious! Kids are sayin' you're racist. You're gonna get suspended, or the black kids are gonna jump you.*

It was well known that many nonwhites, particularly the Mestizo and black kids, would threaten and beat up any white kid who wasn't deferential to them. Anything beyond a failure to be deferential, such as showing pride in one's white identity and Western Culture, was like striking a match in a vapor-rich gas tank: Nonwhites would go into raucous mock injury and eruptions of rage.

And yet, despite the hazards, I felt compelled to press on. Though terrified of being jumped and bloodied, I figured I could fly below the radar, get my questions answered, and maybe do a bit of good for my people in the process.

Crucible

I was asking for so little. My objections were so small. I felt I wouldn't be targeted.

As early in life as my peers and I could be indoctrinated, the entertainment media and educational systems had taught us that to disagree with antiwhite dictates was to be ignorant and backward, hateful and depraved, worthy of scorn and condemnation, and yet I was unprepared for the firestorm that followed my questions.

I was isolated within days and hated within weeks. With the exception of my closest friends, fear of the smear and fear of antiwhite violence drove most of the boys from me. They didn't hate me; they were afraid of me—or rather, afraid of my opinions, afraid of all the cruel ideas and evil personas the Regime, through the media and educational systems, had calculatingly linked to the wellbeing of our people.

But the boys avoiding me was trite compared to the behavior of the white girls; many of them detested me. To them, I was an outcast, and they made sure I knew it by chastising me, by burning me down with contemptuous glares.

Everyone knows how badly we treated them, the white girls scathingly tried to shame me, so young and already so well versed in antiwhite catechisms. *We owe them—what's wrong with you—don't you get it?!*

These eleven to thirteen-year-old white-guilted girls acted like they knew exactly who I was, like they had seen my *type* before. To them, I was suddenly a "neo-Nazi," a "Klan" member with a long dark history of violence and criminal behavior.

Chapter 11 — *Heretic*

Their stares were unceasing and caustic. They made it unmistakably known that I was kicked out of humanity, that I was despised for holding unauthorized opinions. I was in a state of shock. I couldn't reconcile my questions with the hatred directed against me.

And just when the sting of their hate sank into my heart, a message crippled me with fear: Nonwhite 8th graders were angry over my suggestion that a portrait of Lee or Jefferson hang in the Commons—and they were going to *beat me down*.

I had no idea who these "tolerance enforcers" were, but I had every reason to believe their threats. Not only did the school's leftist administration seldom punish students who got into fights, typically just pulling them apart and sending them to class, but fighting garnered status—especially when it was for a "righteous" cause.

Terror wrapped her cold arms around me as I realized I was being hunted by unseen predators. I knew it was only a matter of time before they found me.

Chapter 12

Forsaken

He turned his head in my direction—I was sure he had seen me—but he kept walking.

Brian! Hey Brian! I shouted again over the inter-period babble in the Commons.

He probably didn't see us, offered Greg reassuringly.

Let's catch up with him.

No.... You go ahead. I'm goin' to class, he mumbled, throwing his long, rich hair over his shoulder, drawing the attention and jealousy of a cluster of girls.

All right—see ya, and I took off after Brian, only to stop and spin around a moment later as I remembered to ask Greg about our plans to hang out.

We still hanging out on Friday? I yelled after him.

Turning halfway around while disappearing into the crowd, he hollered back.

Yeah maybe. I'll let you know.

Cool. See you after gym.

Dashing between kids like I was slicing across the basketball court, I pulled alongside Brian a moment later.

What's up?

Hey, he said unenthusiastically, throwing a worried glance at the scuttling throng behind us.

Chapter 12   *Forsaken*

What's wrong—are you sick?

No...I'm fine. Just...going to class, he said distantly, shrugging his shoulders.

Are we still going to your grandparents' this weekend? I asked hopefully.

Brian and I had gone four-wheeling on his grandparents' farm since our legs were long enough to reach the gear shifter.

Yeah. Ted and John (Brian's older brother and his friend) *are gonna be out there. We're gonna play war against 'em*, said Brian, seeming much more like himself.

Awesome! We're gonna kick their asses—like always!

Unfortunately, my excitement about the coming weekend was spoiled by confusion the very next period. While probing for the names of the nonwhites who had promised to beat me down, I realized my comments had reached them by way of my white peers.

Why would they tell them? I asked myself, utterly confused. *Why tell them that I care about how we're treated when they know it'll piss them off—when they know they'll beat me up for it?*

I felt an unexpected sickness when I realized that I had been betrayed by my own people.

How could they do this? I numbly continued, shock creeping over me like ice over a lake. *How could they sell me out? How could they sell me out when I'm only doing this for us? Why can't we stick together, like the nonwhites?*

I was beginning to feel like I was spiraling down a long dark hole: The boys dodged me. My closest friends were acting distant. The white girls who didn't avoid me viewed and treated me as a social outcast, hating me for being a "hater." And worst of all, I walked the halls shadowed by a faceless threat that could strike at any moment—from any direction.

Every night I had nightmares of being jumped and beat-down. Every day I trekked to and from my classes in perpetual terror, constantly looking over my shoulder, constantly gauging faces for aggression.

There was disgrace in seeking help from the administration and teachers. Everyone knew that. Everyone knew that only babies and wimps asked for help, but I had no choice—everyone was against me. I could either wait until I was attacked and beaten bloody, or I could save myself by permanently ruining my reputation, by becoming known as a sissy.

My reputation was important, but my fear of being jumped was crippling.

Some kids want to fight me, I urgently exclaimed to half a dozen teachers and office administrators over as many days.

Who wants to fight you? they queried, concern coloring their features and tones.

I'm not sure who, but I can tell you the names of the kids who'll know. I know they're 8th graders.

Why do they want to fight you?

Chapter 12   *Forsaken*

They don't like that I asked for a portrait of Lee or Jefferson to be hung in the Commons.

Ohhh…well…Jason…. their tones and features would change, becoming flat and awkward. *You need to understand—that's a very emotional subject for some. You'd do better not to talk about it anymore,* they would finish, unconcernedly dismissing me or walking away.

Why won't they help me?! my thoughts fearfully cried as I became increasingly panic-stricken and paralyzed. *Why don't they care about me?! Why won't they look into this—talk to those 8th graders?! Why won't they stop this?! Why tell ME to shut up?!*

Chapter 13

Despair

You haven't been able to do anything…why can't you hang out anymore? I complained to Kevin, anxiously waiting for his response.

We were standing by the lunchroom doors prior to the start of the period, kids noisily spilling into and out of the cafeteria.

I don't know, dude—I'm just busy, he answered with a frown, walking backward and turning on his heel, leaving when the conversation clearly wasn't over.

I stood there in disbelief, my mouth open, my palms forward at my hips in an expression of deep confusion.

My world was crumbling around me. I had never felt more alone, more despised. Terrified and out of options, I slumped against the wall, something deflating inside me.

I can't do it anymore. I can't take it. My only problem is how I'm going to backtrack—how I'm going to distance myself from what I said.

Fortunately, I wasn't being called a sissy; my teachers and the administration hadn't taken any steps to investigate or confront the 8th graders who threatened to beat me down, so no one knew I had asked them for help. But beyond that, and my continuing successes on the football field, everything in my life was falling apart.

Jason, said a melodious voice to my left, *are you all right?*

Chapter 13   *Despair*

Fine...yes, I began, looking up into Mrs. Peyton's concerned blue eyes.

She set a hand on my shoulder and pursed her lips consolingly.

Are you sure something isn't bothering you?

No, I'm...I'm fine, I lied, nodding and putting on a fake smile.

If you say so, she sighed, eyeing me disbelievingly.

Where are all your friends? You're normally with a group of boys.

They're coming, I continued lying.

There was simply no use in telling her that my life had fallen apart in the blink of an eye. There was nothing she could do about it.

If you're having any problems, Jason, she squeezed my shoulder supportively, *you know you can approach any of the adults in this school.*

Yeah—I know. I'm fine. I was just thinking.

Okay, she said brightly, her smile briefly filling me with a warm joy that gave way to a cold emptiness the moment she strolled away.

I slouched into the cafeteria and found a seat where I wouldn't be ignored or the table abandoned as soon as I sat down.

Having no appetite, I mechanically dragged my lunch from my paper bag: PB&J, cheese and crackers, Capri Sun. Every bite was bland, and every swallow landed in my stomach like lead ingots.

As I mournfully listened to the merriment around me, noting smiles and laughter with a deep, longing pain, I speculated that if I disavowed my statements, I could avert my beat-down—that was my most pressing concern. I also hoped that doing so would put an end to my banishment: My friends would speak to me again, and the white girls would abandon their campaign to blame and shame me.

I'll say that I really don't care about white people...that I really don't care about the portraits...that it was a dumb idea...that I was just playing...I'll tell them I think Martin Luther King was the greatest American ever...I'll tell them I'm sorry...that I've never been sorrier about anything in all my life....

I dropped my PB&J on the table and scanned the lunchroom from my solitary prison.

Stuffing my uneaten food back in my lunch bag, I said decisively, *That's it. That's what I'll do.*

Chapter 14

Shunned

He wrote his name on the white-board and turned around.

Mrs. Johnson will be about fifteen minutes late today, so I'm standing in for her until she arrives. I'll be taking attendance, and then you all will begin—he glanced down at a small yellow tablet—*or will continue reading Chapter 3 to yourselves. Obviously, there'll be no talking, or I'll be forced to make you stand on your heads,* he finished with a wry frown.

A few giggled at the absurdity of Mr. Albright's warning—even I chuckled in spite of the way I felt.

Today was the first time I'd seen him since he chased me and my friends out of the theater. His affable nature made it easy to relax, which was a welcome reprieve from the pain of ostracism and the fear of beat-down.

But my anxiety returned the very next minute as my thoughts went painfully back to my plan to redeem myself. I had tried for three days to profess my new opinions, but I couldn't do it. I simply couldn't make myself say that I didn't care about my people and the portraits, that I thought MLK was the greatest of all Americans.

I was torn between two poles: On the one hand, I wanted to be accepted, I wanted to be liked, I wanted to be included; and on the other hand, I was driven by a passion that was unquenchable in its contempt for every thought that asked me to betray my people.

Jason Köhne?

Albright had read my name from the attendance sheet and was scanning the room.

Here—I raised my hand.

Oh—Jason Köhne, is it? We meet again.

I grinned sheepishly, the class turning their faces toward me in deep curiosity.

Diego Flores? Albright continued, unperturbed, and the class—thankfully—released me from its questioning gaze.

The room's silence and the soft crackle of turning pages painfully swelled the gloomy sea in which I was drowning. I couldn't focus. I couldn't concentrate on anything but the prospect of my beat-down and my crumbling friendships. And that's when I realized, with a terrifying jolt that clinched my fingers painfully into my textbook, that if Fox had heard about my stance, she would never have anything to do with me.

I desperately wanted her to like me, and now—racked by a cold, confused sweat—I wondered whether or not she hated me. I had to know—somehow—if she knew. And if she knew, I had to find a way to make up for it.

Mrs. Johnson bustled into the room ten minutes later, startling me out of my panicked concern over Fox's opinion.

Ethan, thank you—I owe you.

No, you don't. He closed the novel he was reading and rose from behind the desk. *Everyone is accounted for, but*—he ran his

Chapter 14 *Shunned*

finger down the attendance sheet—*Dwain Carter was five minutes late.*

Okay—I'll handle it.

Turning her attention to the class, she raised her voice. *Everyone—quickly pick a partner for the project we discussed last week.*

As Mrs. Johnson and Mr. Albright said their goodbyes, everyone scrambled to find partners. Noticing that Greg was edging over to a boy named Scott without a single glance in my direction, I turned to Ian as he was being turned down by the kid beside him.

You want to be partners? I asked.

Umm... he threw a sleepy glance across the room, *I was going to ask...hold on.*

He got up and walked across the room before pulling up short when he saw that whoever he was going to ask already had a partner.

What's he doing? I thought to myself, injured by his behavior.

I guess he's gotta partner with me now.

But on his way back, he asked Tina to be his partner.

Purposefully avoiding my stunned expression, he stiltedly trudged over to retrieve his books so he could join her at her desk.

Tina? The girl you call tubby Tina?

I had to find a partner, didn't I? He shrugged and walked away.

Does anyone not have a partner? asked Mrs. Johnson over the buzz of the room, causing everyone to go silent.

I don't, I raised my hand into the empty air, the only one in the room—alone.

Chapter 15

Collision Course

I desperately wanted to prevent my beat-down and to redeem myself with my peers. I wanted to get back where I was, back with my friends, back when things were going right, back before I had to constantly worry about being attacked.

My inability to disavow my people had frustrated my plans to redeem myself, but I thought I had found a solution the following week when I decided to quietly abandon my portrait campaign, and to wear sweatpants to school like some of the cool and black kids. I had hoped that by disappearing in the crowd my earlier statements would be forgotten.

Unfortunately, while I had no problem wearing sweatpants and dropping the portrait issue, it was impossible to stop myself from speaking in defense of my people. Whether it was listening to a lecture, or watching a movie, or reading a textbook, or having a conversation, I was simply unable to tolerate most antiwhite remarks.

Why would I owe Lamar anything? I innocently blurted in class, as Lamar, startled by the mention of his name, listened from two seats over. *I didn't own slaves and he wasn't one. I ate dinner at his house last year. His family owns a bigger house and nicer cars than mine!*

That doesn't matter, indignantly spat my teacher, Mrs. Barr, as the boys in the room cast their eyes in fear to the floor, and some of the girls attempted to slay me—Medusa-like—with theirs. All of which further inflamed my sense of justice.

Black Americans were historically mistreated—

Carl's mom drives a shiny BMW, I interrupted, jabbing a thumb over my shoulder in Carl's direction (a black boy in the back of the class). *And my mom drives a used station wagon.*

I told you, that doesn't matter!

It would matter if it were my family with the nicer cars and bigger house, wouldn't it?

That's enough! she said in a dangerous voice, her hands on her hips and color rising in her ugly, round face.

I glanced across the room at Mark for support—he had stopped sitting beside me days earlier—but he averted his eyes.

Well—I turned my attention back to Barr—*when won't we owe them anymore?*

One more word and I'll send you to the office, fiercely threatened the classroom priestess of antiwhitism.

The rumors of my imminent beat-down grew steadily. The most terrifying parts of my day were the periods between classes and during lunch; that's when they would jump me.

The weight of a thousand fears fell from my shoulders every time I made it to class without being attacked. But fear quickly dragged my eyes to the clock's hands, forcing me to dread the bell that signaled the return of the threat that hunted me in the halls, subjecting me to the whim of chance and the bloodlust of the antiwhites.

Chapter 15 *Collision Course*

While my father—a construction worker, who was more durable than hardened steel—had shared a couple tips on how to make a fist and throw a punch the previous summer, I had never been in a fight. The mere thought made me lightheaded and weak-kneed.

Sure, I was athletic—a star athlete—and I was strong, as my father had encouraged me to join him in a regimen of sit-ups and pushups every other night since I was six years old, but the nonwhite 8th graders were double my level of physical maturity.

More importantly, I had already seen several fights in the halls, and they had seared a lasting impression on me. The fighters were fierce, they were merciless, and I was certain—well out of my league.

Chapter 16

Alone

He wouldn't return my calls. He wouldn't seek me out at lunch or in the Commons. He wouldn't have anything to say when I tried to talk to him. He wouldn't even look at me. My first and only best friend in my whole life had left me.

I still saw Brian at school, but our deep bond and friendship was over. I had never been so heartbroken.

Greg, Ian, Kevin, and Mark still said hello, but that was it. Only Adam and Chris occasionally spoke to me, but they kept it short, always casting a wary eye for who was watching.

My thoughts were my only companions, and they tormented me with fear and sadness. I was shunned. I was hated. I was alone.

Chapter 17

Inquisition

Mr. Cribbs will see you, said a secretary indifferently as she plucked the phone off its base—*sorry for keeping you on hold*....

Moments earlier, an 8th grader had come to my class carrying a slip of paper, which he presented to my teacher with a self-important flourish. Under the inquisitive gaze of the entire class, she silently read it and then called me to her desk, instructing me to bring my things.

With the class's intense scrutiny probing like hungry fingers over and around my shoulders, she informed me that the vice principal wanted to speak with me. I had nervously followed the 8th grader past the all-seeing Idol and on to the school's office, where I tensely waited for 15 minutes on the edge of a brown, faux-leather couch.

I had never been in trouble at school. I had never been summoned to the office. I was terrified.

Standing there with no idea of where to go after the secretary's curt announcement, I was about to ask where his office was when Vice Principal Cribbs bustled out of a short hallway, his tan suit flapping animatedly in the breeze of his hurried movements.

Mr. Köhne —come with me, he ordered flatly, a grim look on his face.

He motioned for me to sit down as he dropped himself into a handsome desk chair, causing it to roll smoothly along the carpeted floor.

His office smelled thickly of coconut body-lotion. The florescent ceiling-lights, which lighted every other office, were turned off in favor of two lamps. The first was ornate, glass-shaded and perched on an end table beside my chair. The second was on his desk: green and brass, as is often seen in lawyers' offices on television. Aside from the theater, his was the dimmest room I had ever seen in a school.

Mr. Köhne, it has come to my attention that you're stirring up trouble by suggesting the school display portraits of slave owners alongside Dr. King.

His eyes shone with a cold seriousness as though he were a judge, the crime murder, and the penalty death.

No…I mean yes…I did…Robert E. Lee and Thomas Jefferson. But I don't want that anymore. I just thought it would be fair—

Fair? he barked loudly, startling me. *That wouldn't be fair to the minority students at this school.*

Holding me with a dark-brown gaze, he leaned thoughtfully back in his chair, sitting forward the next moment as something on his desk caught his eye, utterly diverting his attention as he rapidly leafed through some documents.

Maybe we could have Lee or Jefferson on the other side of the Commons?

His head shot up as though surprised by my presence, an amused smile leaping across his face.

Absolutely not, he laughed loudly and merrily as if I had asked him to display portraits of the Easter Bunny and Santa Claus.

Chapter 17   *Inquisition*

    A quiet knock and his office door swung open; a casually dressed, curly-haired man stepped inside, whom I recognized at once.

    Jason, this is Mr. Wolf; he's the school's guidance director. I've asked him to join us, said Cribbs, smoothing his lapels and sighing mirthfully to himself.

    Mr. Wolf sank into the plush chair to my right.

    Where are we?

    Mr. Köhne just suggested that we hang portraits of Lee and Jefferson on the other side of the Commons—a faceoff with Dr. King. What do you think?

    Now seeming in good spirits, he chuckled and smiled at Wolf the way friends do when they're sharing an inside joke.

    Wolf shook his head and pursed his lips. *You're in for a tough time young man.*

    I don't want that anymore, I blurted, suddenly noticing that my hands were shaking, terrified that I was about to be suspended or expelled.

    I called you down here because I wanted to put an end to this nonsense, said Cribbs. *We will never hang their portraits. Is that understood?*

    Yes sir, I answered.

    I also wanted to address that several of your teachers have informed me that you've been disrupting class with questions of a racist nature.

    What's going on, Jason? asked Wolf, tilting his head and narrowing his brow.

I've not…I'm just…nothing…they misunderstood me.

I was shocked that my teachers had gone to the administration over my questions, but—more than that—I was horrified because I suddenly realized that they hadn't misunderstood me, they had misrepresented me.

We take these sorts of things seriously, Jason. There's no place for it in school, said Wolf with a patronizing grin.

There are kids who want to beat me up, I blurted, half wanting to change the subject, half wanting to get their help.

Speaking through a snicker, Cribbs said, *I bet kids want to fight you over comments like that.*

Wolf leaned in toward me, taking an affectedly deep breath.

Jason, if you drop all this, I'm sure it'll be fine, he said in a tone of mock concern.

My eyes bounced between the two of them: Cribbs smiling as though he were recovering from the funniest joke he had ever heard, Wolf grinning like he had cornered dinner.

Okay, I intoned softly, nodding, and at a complete loss of what to say.

Wolf stood and patted me on the shoulder. *The bell's about to ring, so don't bother going back to class. Just sit in the office until the period's over.*

Chapter 18

Talons

Shuffling to class down this crowded hallway had its drawbacks, but it also had its benefits. I hated the crowd, but the crowd made me feel less conspicuous. And more importantly, I always got to see one of the members of The Triad strolling in the opposite direction. I didn't know her name but she was every bit as pretty as Fox.

Fox…god—I wonder if she's heard anything bad about me, I worriedly asked myself as I moped along. *I'm sure she'll never like me if she has. I need to find out what she—*

That's the little racist! a boy excitedly shouted.

Confusedly stirring out of my internal dialogue, I alarmingly noticed face after face searching me as though expecting to find horns or infected sores.

The world became dreamlike as an area opened in the throng of students by a set of large, chestnut doors: gates through which I had to pass.

Before those doors were two 8th graders—a Mestizo and an Asian. Wearing venomous grins, they were uniformed as wannabe rappers, the Mestizo kid sucking on a blood-red lollypop as they mocked me.

Yeah that's him, said the lollypop sucker through red-stained lips while passers-by slowed to a halt to watch the exchange.

Crucible

My mouth and eyes gaped. A panicked voice in my head urged me to run, but I couldn't move. I just stood there atop legs I couldn't feel, helplessly watching as the crowd made space around us.

Are these the ones?! my thoughts anxiously screamed. *Oh my god, is this it?! Is this the beat-down?!*

What you got to say now? jeeringly demanded the Asian boy as the walls drew in upon me like a trap, and nameless students turned on me with blank faces, waiting for my response.

But I didn't answer him. I couldn't even think beyond the word "racist"; I had never been called a racist before. The word was a weapon—value-loaded to such an extent that it struck me like a hammer: In movie after movie, TV show after TV show, class after class, we were taught that a racist was evil, ugly, stupid, cruel, bestial, wicked—white.

I wanted to speak. I wanted to defend myself by saying I wasn't a racist, that all I wanted was dignity for my people, but fear paralyzed my mouth.

Dread gathered around me as the Asian kid got in my face. Bumping his chest into mine and leering threateningly down his nose, he berated me as the lollypop sucker barked with red-lipped laughter.

You got a problem with me? Because I ain't white?! Huh?! Mother-fucker! Huh?! I ought'a beat your shit, he sprayed, a fanatical blaze in his dark eyes, the heads of the crowd tracking the insults and their impact like a bowling ball on helpless pins.

I heard a loud clap, my vision went white and came back, my cheek stinging: He had punched or slapped me.

Chapter 18 *Talons*

What you got? Huh? Huh? he shouted, wildly throwing his arms out to his sides.

My mind was blank. Nothing came to me; no ideas of what to say or do—nothing…not until—a lesson my father had shared: *A man never fights when he doesn't have to, son. But in this world, you'll come across people who want nothing more than to hurt you and your family, and when you do—you've got to get the jaws. You've got to hurt 'em first. Don't worry, you won't have to guess who they are; you'll know 'em when you see 'em.*

At last, I had my response: Fury filled me. My jaw tightened. My fists clenched. A moment later and my book-bag fell from my shoulder as my fist crashed into his face.

My knuckles landed high on his left cheek, but it was enough, as providence had come to my aid. Tripping as he stepped backward from the blow, he fell to the floor, bouncing his head off the hard tile. He struggled to get to his feet, his limbs flailing, but I was too scared to let him rise; I knew he'd finish me.

I stepped forward and slapped his hands aside to get another shot on his face.

Stop! Stop! he squealed as he raised his hands in a pitiable appeal for clemency, his face screwed into agony, the crowd gasping.

The lollypop sucker's high-pitched voice shrieked from somewhere behind me. *Stop! Stop it! Fuckin'-A, asshole!*

I stepped back, numb and stunned by what had just happened. Grabbing my book-bag and keeping my eyes on the two of them, I backtracked my way down the hall. I couldn't remember which way I

Crucible

had to go or even what class I was supposed to attend, but I knew the tardy-bell was imminent.

We're gonna get you mother-fucker! one of them shouted as I hustled toward the Commons. They would surely come after me now—

Fighting the urge to cry and struggling not to vomit, I burst into the Commons. There, trembling, I dropped to my knees and fumbled through my papers, desperately searching for my class schedule. But it was hopeless. I couldn't think straight. I couldn't even decipher the words on the papers I frantically tore from my book-bag—and then the tardy-bell rang.

Chapter 18   *Talons*

In the deserted stillness that followed, I realized that I had no friends, that I was surrounded by antiwhites who hated me. I was trembling when I felt the warm tears trickle down my face: a white child, groping for his class schedule, hunted by the self-proclaimed champions of "tolerance" and "brotherhood," haunted by antiwhite teachers and admin—a speck of dust in the Commons beneath the silent, towering image of the Idol.

Chapter 19

Persistence

In the battle-laden halls of my junior high, accounts of fights spread with an ease that shamed the common cold.

If I had been unknown to most of the violent zealots of antiwhitism, if I had been nothing more than a day's gossip, I would have been happy, but I feared my popularity had grown among my victimizers. I feared that the punch I had thrown in self-defense would inspire more antiwhites to deliver the beat-down they claimed I "deserved" for holding prohibited opinions. I didn't even know if the Asian boy had made the original threats, which left me with no alternative but to conclude I was still being hunted.

I remained vigilant even though things were quietly changing in the ensuing weeks. My MVP year on the football field had done wonders for my likability. My friends hadn't returned, but more kids spoke to me as my reputation subtly shifted from *Jason the racist* to *Jason the great athlete*.

Amid the smiles from unknown girls and the approving nods of adults, amid the praise and admiration of the jocks, I was tempted to deny myself, to turn my back on my identity, to repudiate every thought that had led to my previous—hated—persona.

This is my way out! I thought to myself repeatedly.

My darkness was becoming day. Why go back? Why instigate my victimizers? Why put myself in the position of being hated and

Chapter 19 *Persistence*

beat-down by the self-named advocates of "anti-hate" and "non-violence?" The school was too big for a twelve-year-old boy to change. Why not just bask in the glow of my athletic achievements?

And so I decided to keep my mouth shut. I bit my tongue. Antiwhitism made me furious, but things were different now. I was becoming a bit of a celebrity. I was beginning to feel as high as I had felt low.

Nothing was going to make me go back to that horrid place (those feelings, that isolation, that bleak future), nothing—except perhaps the endless antiwhite provocations: the insults, the smears, the blackened heritage I was forced to wear like a shroud of penitence, the self-flagellation that I was expected to perform, the disgust that I was required to feel for my people.

I wanted to be liked! I wanted to have friends again! But the antiwhites denied my people dignity, they denied them an identity and a future. I was torn to pieces by my desire to be accepted and the spirit that moved within me, compelling me to defend the dignity of my people, to fight for the pride and wellbeing of my own kind.

Ms. Stark said you were disrupting class with provocative questions, began Mr. Cribbs airily, checking the time on his sparkling wristwatch as we sat in his dim office.

I'm tired of hearing about whites hurting Jews…about how Jews are always the innocent victims and how they never do anything wrong…. Jews have hurt whites, too, I respectfully protested, as Cribbs, half listening, reclined in his chair and threw his hands behind his head, a potbelly leaping over his belt as his brown suit-jacket fell open. *Besides, if anybody owes anyone, it's the Jews who owe whites; it was white people who saved the Jews in World War II.*

No, it wasn't! bleated Cribbs as he abruptly came to life, laughing disbelievingly and leaning forward, pearly white teeth spreading across his dark, mirthful face. *It was a multicultural effort that freed Europe from Nazism.*

Jason, I don't know where you get these—ideas (he stretched the word with a face that looked as though he were pulling something unsavory from his mouth), *but even if you disagree with the curriculum you'll have to come to terms with what's taught here. I'm giving you an hour of detention. Now, I don't expect to see you in my office again*, he added stiffly, pointing unceremoniously to the door.

Chapter 20

Logic

Two things remained unchanged for me: In some small measure, I was still an advocate for my people's wellbeing, and the white girls who suffered most severely from white-guilt continued to despise me.

No matter where I crossed the gaze of these "champions of compassion," they never spared me the cruelest glares, or the equally spiteful refusals to acknowledge my existence.

That's so racist, they would hiss, their eyes flashing with cultish fanaticism. *You don't care about their suffering!*

And you don't care about OUR suffering, I would retort, undaunted by their antiwhite zeal.

We don't suffer. We have everything. Look at how good we have it! they would fume reproachfully, blushing scarlet. *But just look around the world and see how poor and miserable they are. We did that to them! Nothing else can explain the differences! We stole everything from them!*

That doesn't make any sense. The things that make up Western Civilization would have to exist elsewhere for us to have stolen them. And they don't! No one else builds Western Civilization. Besides, I didn't do anything to them—and neither did you. We don't owe them a thing.

Their behavior was unnatural. It struck me as diseased. Any animal, I concluded, hostile to the survival of its own kind could only be considered diseased.

If a group of doves chased other doves from the things they needed to survive—like water—food—shelter (I ticked on my fingers) *so that pigeons could have those things, wouldn't we say those doves were crazy? We're being forced to give up our country, culture, and language, and what's worse is that we're not even allowed to decide who we are*, I told a group of six or seven semi-attentive listeners at a lunch table after a sleep-inducing lecture that turned corrosively antiwhite the previous period.

Truuuue…but we're not animals, conceitedly snapped a red-headed girl in response, while Mr. Albright passed our table with two black boys wearing scowls like Halloween masks tied to their heads, escorting them from the cafeteria.

And besides, she continued bitchily, *we're all humans—just different skin.*

Well they're all birds—just different feathers, I countered. *And even if you don't think we're animals, we live and die like animals, don't we?* I asked the group.

A few at the table, shrugging their shoulders and frowning, nodded reluctant agreement.

Whites who think like those doves are sick, I adamantly opined, searching my listeners' faces for any glimmer of agreement.

My mom and dad say that everything'll be fine once we make up to the minorities, declared a drab girl in a tone of self-importance, nodding sharply at the end of her statement as though punctuating an irrefutable truism.

No! It won't be fine. We're not talking about two people—where one can make up something to the other. God! We're talking about a storyline. The white kids before us were the bad guys, and now we're the bad guys, and the white kids after us will be the bad guys—it's a storyline. It won't change unless we change it.

Though the girls had nothing to say in response, the remainder of the kids at the table shrugged their shoulders, and then the two girls, sharing an agreeing glance, got up and left.

I was dumbfounded by their determined stupidity and dogged self-deception. But I was also frustrated, because, like many of the boys, I increasingly felt the need for female approval and attention.

I wanted the girls to like me, to smile at me and laugh with me. I wanted them to say my name and wave when they saw me. But as my post-season football fame waned, my smiles were scorned by the girls, my hellos went unrequited, my feelings were trampled upon. Their aversion was heart-wrenching.

It may be—I speculated one mournful evening, trying to understand their behavior—that most females are more naturally inclined to feel guilty in certain situations. I always noticed that the girls seemed far more troubled by the claims of nonwhite suffering—particularly the claims that focused on nonwhite children.

The white girls' faces would contort with grief. Many of them would clap their hands to their mouths, or wring their hands in their laps. Maybe these were the incipient signs of instinct, of mothering, of protecting the weak and the defenseless—as nonwhites (no matter how violent) were endlessly portrayed to be. And perhaps this is why they hated those—such as myself—who showed concern for those whom the antiwhites victimized as the "victimizers."

It may be—I also speculated—that most females are more naturally inclined to concern themselves with the perceived opinions of others. I observed that most girls were very concerned with fashion. But this concern for fashion went well beyond attire, hair, and makeup. Most girls seemed far—FAR more concerned with holding fashionable opinions than most boys.

And who decides what's fashionable? If we're talking about attire, we might say companies in New York and Paris make these "weighty" and lucrative decisions. But if we're talking about ideological fashion—well—the Regime decides: The most powerful people determine what serves their agenda, and that becomes ideological fashion.

Perhaps this is why so many of the girls turned up their fashion-conscious noses at people like me: I held what the Regime deemed were the most unfashionable ideas—the ideological bell bottoms of the ages.

This new desire for female attention was like nothing I had ever experienced. It swelled and rose like a liquid fire kindled deep within me: organic, instinctual, it consumed my thoughts and threatened to tear down every obstacle, even the defense of my people.

Everywhere I turned, I saw boys surrendering to this desire—and I wanted to be one of them. The girls suffered no one who spoke

Chapter 20   *Logic*

out against the Regime's antiwhite ideology. They gave no time to boys they perceived to be ideologically unfashionable.

In response to the girls' conditions for approval, the boys modified their opinions so as not to affront them. It was a cruel dynamic: The girls, grossly afflicted with white-guilt and overly concerned with the opinions deemed fashionable by the Regime, induced the boys to fake (and even genuinely adopt in some cases) antiwhite opinions. Most of the girls were simply incapable of seeing through the Regime's ruse, and most of the boys couldn't have cared less.

I was trapped, spurred by a new instinct to repeatedly reevaluate my loyalty to my people, and when I found no reconciliation of the two—I sank further into grief. But my brooding was always interrupted: Antiwhitism continually stirred me to anger with endless provocations, and the loudly self-proclaimed "humanitarians" continually threatened to inhumanely punish me for my lack of devotion to antiwhite precepts.

Chapter 21

Native

The final bell of the week had mercifully rung moments earlier.

Unable to stem the tide, I hugged the wall and inched along when Adam's voice sailed over the jubilant noise.

Where you going? hollered Adam, as he and Chris angled over to me amid the rush of kids leaving the building.

I have after-school tutoring with Mrs. Swan.

Sorry about that, sympathized Chris, looking down at me from last summer's growth spurt, still seeming like he was about to topple over.

No, it's fine. I like Mrs. Swan.

Has anybody tried fighting you since I talked to you on...what was it, Tuesday, Wednesday? asked Chris.

No. Thank God.

There were some kids talking bad about you earlier today, revealed Adam, worriedly searching the cheerful and laughing faces that scurried by us.

What did they say?

One of 'em said that you said whites are natives.

We are natives. I did say that. I'm sick of hearing that we're invaders. I was born here, my parents were born here, my grandparents, great-grandparents, great-great-grandparents—and

Chapter 21   *Native*

who knows how much further back—they were all born here. And every generation has served in the military. Whites invented America! Whites—are—natives.

That's true! agreed Chris emphatically.

Rare, and in private though it was, I was always happy to hear Chris and Adam agree with me. I looked meaningfully at him before continuing.

The same people who say this country isn't ours—are the same ones that say that an illegal Mexican who's been here five minutes is an American, and that his claim to OUR inheritance is legit. And I don't care what the teachers say; whites aren't immigrants. What country did we immigrate to? I disgustedly spat.

Whites are pioneers. The people who came here and the people we brought here after we built the country—they're the immigrants. You know what (I was becoming animated, attracting the attention of passers-by)*—I'm really starting to think the teachers and admin know exactly what they're doing to us. You know what I mean? Like, what they're doing isn't an accident at all.*

I know, man—I agree—I just don't want anyone else to know I agree, said Adam with a nervous chuckle, bouncing on his toes and looking up at Chris, who agreeingly nodded and grinned back. *I'm just telling you because some kids were saying that you needed your ass kicked because you said that.*

Great! Well, I guess they're gonna have to get in line.

Don't worry about it, said Chris bracingly. *Kids talk shit all the time.*

I don't think you should say anything else…it doesn't help. You said you were gonna stop—said Adam in a nervous, questioning tone.

I am. I'm gonna stop because it's not worth it. Nobody cares. I'm just hated for it. It's just hard sometimes, you know? I don't want to say anything because I don't want everyone hating me and wanting to kick my ass, but sometimes I just can't take the double standards and the bashing.

Yeah, we hate it, too, agreed Chris. *We're just not as brave as you.*

Anyhow, I took a deep breath, *did you guys find out anything about Fox?*

Adam frowned. *Nope, sorry.*

Chris shook his head apologetically.

If you guys can—just—PLEASE—find out if she's said anything about me…ask her friend…Megan, or whatever her name is…you guys know her, right?

Yeah, we'll ask her, Adam said honestly as Greg, Ian, and Kevin walked by, ignoring us.

I silently and sadly watched them pass before turning back to Adam and Chris, both of whom were frowning sympathetically. *Thanks, guys. I better get going, or Mrs. Swan will leave.*

When I entered the library, I found Mrs. Swan waiting in the eerie stillness that always filled the building after school let out. She beamed at me as I approached.

Chapter 21   *Native*

We worked on my homework for about thirty minutes before she suddenly went stiff, telling me in a serious voice that she wanted to ask me a question.

Jason, are you having problems at home?

No. Why? I said, noticing a librarian quietly moving among the bookshelves.

Her question made me feel nervous and self-conscious.

You started the year with such good grades…and you were happier and enthusiastic…your grades—they've really fallen—and you're always alone when I see you. What's going on?

No…everything's good, I lied, curling my toes in my shoes.

She gave me a tragic look.

I've heard you've been having some problems in class—you've been asking a lot of emotive questions.

Yeah, I mumbled, but I wanted to say that it was difficult to be silent when I was endlessly insulted by antiwhite remarks, and that it was impossible to concentrate on my studies when I was constantly afraid that I was about to be beaten down.

No longer able to look her in the eyes, I intently studied my pencil. I knew what was coming—another lecture on how everybody's the same and how important and virtuous it is for us to be deferential to nonwhites. I had heard the same lecture scores of times in my short life.

You might want to cool that down until your grades recover.

I know. I am. I'm stopping, I said to my pencil.

Crucible

  She began packing up her things, which clearly meant we were done for the day.

  On my lonely walk home, I reaffirmed my resolution to ignore antiwhitism, refocusing my energies on my studies. Little did I know that in the coming weeks my school work was going to be the last thing on my mind.

Chapter 22

Death Threat

Enduring the antiwhite verbal abuse in silence was torturous, but the pretexts, inconsistencies, illogicality, inescapable antiwhite conclusions, and my teachers' bogus impartiality were driven violently from my mind when I was told that a black boy's cousin—fresh from juvenile detention—was going to *kill* me if he ever caught me walking home from school.

...he just got out of juvie, Jason. They say he stabbed somebody. He's like, 14 or something, and really good at fighting, I was told by those who acted concerned as well as those who enjoyed terrorizing me.

Was this the *monster* Adam had warned me about when I started down this path—the one to whom my questions would warrant unspeakable violence? Could Adam's fears have become my fate? Could the word *monster* have leapt out at me because somewhere deep down, somewhere in my core, I felt—I knew—that the incessant antiwhite message propagated throughout society spawned such people?

The threat of being murdered for my opinions paralyzed me. Desperate and alone, I turned (again) to my teachers and administration for help.

Kids still talk about fighting me all the time, and now some black kid's cousin says he's gonna KILL me on my way home from school, I frantically informed them. *You've got to do something! You've got to help me!*

Their responses were nightmarish:

For heaven's sake, that's ridiculous—nobody is going to fight you.

They're just talking. Nothing's going to happen.

Nobody is going to kill you. That's absurd.

Their anger is understandable. Wouldn't you agree?

Jason, you're bringing all this on yourself.

Only you have the power to stop this.

I needed to do something, but what? Transfer to a different school? My parents had already told me that we'd have to move for me to transfer, and that wasn't going to happen. Tell the police? If the administration and my teachers didn't care, why would the police?

I didn't know how much more I could take. Was I going to be beat-down, and if so, how many beatings would I have to take before the antiwhites were satisfied? Or would their satisfaction depend upon something on the horizon, something much worse than a beat-down?

The administration's and my teachers' refusal to investigate the threats to my life confused, then frightened, and then infuriated me. It was infinitely important to white-guilt me (and all my white peers) for invisible, bogus crimes such as "institutional racism" and "white privilege," but when real, tangible, physical threats were made by nonwhites against me, they viewed it as a trivial matter, instructing me to stop making the "minorities" want to hurt me.

Chapter 22   *Death Threat*

As my fear turned to anger, and anger to determination, I realized I was facing antiwhite terrorism, that no one would help me, and that silence wouldn't atone for my concern for my people.

I knew I was a child, but I was going to have to be a man.

Chapter 23

Righteous

I had refused to feel apologetic for being white. I had refused to accept that my people were evil, deserving of punishment and liable for an eternal compensation. And as I resolved to be a man, to challenge antiwhitism with a new verve and energy, my questions were more direct, my positions were more conspicuous:

If it's good for the nonwhites, it's good for whites.

Every race has enslaved every other race.

If I can't blame nonwhites or their cultures for the crimes that members of their groups commit today, then you can't blame me and my people's culture for crimes committed by whites hundreds and even thousands of years ago!

If black and Mestizo pride are good, then so is white pride.

If bigoted whites control the system, if they're this dominant group that's holding everyone else down, then why do I have to listen to how awful whites are?

If racist whites are in control, then why am I punished for speaking up for whites?

The Regime had created and spread a caricature of a proud white person as hateful and violent, but I was sensitive, mostly introverted, respectful of adults and authority. That made it difficult for my teachers to dismiss my questions, which forced them to respond—to justify the unjustifiable, to defend the indefensible.

Chapter 23 *Righteous*

They struggled, became confused, started and backtracked and started again, changed the subject, resorted to emotional appeals, and lost credibility. In the end, all they could do was define my positions—in so many words—as hateful and dangerous.

As I climbed into my teenage years, my birthday went unnoticed. Most of my peers ignored or hated me. My teachers' thinly disguised revulsion increasingly surfaced as my questions punctured gaping holes in their antiwhite faith. With every day that passed and every question I asked, an antiwhite hatred wrapped a thickening darkness around me.

Jason! D'you know that Martin wants to fight you? gasped a kid I knew from my basketball team, Ryan, after he pulled himself from a boisterous sea of jostling students to reach me.

Who's Martin? I choked, as I halted in the middle of a hallway near the library, utterly taken by surprise, scanning the oblivious crowd at his back as though the threat tore at his heels.

A black kid, panted Ryan, his eyes popping.

What grade?

8th.

Is he coming now? I asked in a shaky voice, my heart thundering a crescendo in my ears, the air unmoving in my lungs.

Yeah! He's looking for you!

Chapter 24

Hunted

Another betrayal by one of my white peers opened the gates to my victimizers.

Days earlier, I had learned that awards were going to be issued to students at the end of the year. Though the school was predominantly white, there was going to be an equal distribution of awards among the races, which meant that we were going to be discriminated against on the basis of our race. There was also going to be an additional set of awards strictly reserved for nonwhite students.

I was furious, and I had spoken on the subject in every class.

If there are nonwhite awards, I conscientiously declared to hostile audiences, *there should be white awards.*

That wouldn't be fair to the minorities…and it would be totally racist, inanely groaned a white girl, rolling her eyes as though I, rather than she, was stupid, her blue-jeans and pea-green turtleneck struggling to restrain her corpulent rolls.

You're gonna get your ass kicked, dude, sneered an 8th grade white boy, shaking his pimple-racked horse-face in disbelief and adding, *whatever!*

This isn't up for discussion, Jason, shot one of my teachers in scandalized tones, her eyes clamping shut like springing mousetraps as she spoke.

Chapter 24 　　　　　　　　 *Hunted*

Jason, said Mr. Wolf disgustedly, *you can't change this. Just go to class and do your schoolwork.*

My demands and my next location had been carried to the ears of a black 8th grader by an antiwhite white boy who was intensely jealous of everyone he perceived as superior to himself.

Ever sensitive to any hint of "inequality," the antiwhite black boy, Martin, decided that my demand for the equal treatment of whites warranted an immediate and violent beat-down.

Yeah! He's looking for you! said Ryan quickly, turning around and feverishly studying the crowd. *There he is!*

At the far end of the hall was a black kid, obviously Martin, purposefully striding in my direction: his fists balled, his chest bowed, his face barbaric. Behind him scrambled a swarm of morbidly obsessed onlookers, mostly white, clearly eager to see what they hoped would be a massacre.

Ryan nervously cleaned the sweat from his palms on the sides of his jeans.

He owns a pair of brass knuckles, too. I've seen 'em. What're you gonna do?

I don't know, I heard myself respond in a shaky voice, unable to tear my eyes from the Idol's "equality" enforcer.

I was terrified and confused. I knew there wasn't a chance in hell of reasoning with Martin, and I didn't want to fight him either, especially if he were wearing brass knuckles. But maybe I didn't have to. He hadn't seen me, and none of the kids around me had any idea a fight was coming.

I think—I think I'll see you later, Ryan, I said in a voice of forced calm, as I stepped through an unlabeled door to my right.

Thanks! I called after him as he perplexedly sped down the hall, casting nervous glances over his shoulder at Martin and his entourage.

Gloomily lit, the room was a musty storage space. Metal shelves lined the walls, cardboard boxes lined the shelves, and computer printouts lined the boxes, through which, one of the school's librarians speedily riffled.

Can I help you, dear? She trilled pleasantly from a warm smile.

Yeah, uh—I was just wondering, I stalled, throwing fearful looks at the open doorway and debating whether or not to tell her that I was about to be jumped. *Do you have a book on the Red Baron?*

I'm sure we do. I'll help you find one, said the warm smile as she strode right by me and entered the hall, walking in Martin's direction—expecting me to follow.

I couldn't think of anything to say to stop her. I couldn't tell her that my feet suddenly weighed hundreds of pounds, or that a violent antiwhite was on his way to beat me down, so I unwillingly, tremblingly followed.

A moment later and the warm smile and I came face-to-face with the angry procession as we wended toward the library.

That's him! shrieked a boy when we neared the group.

Chapter 24   *Hunted*

Uh oh, seems like somebody's looking for trouble, she whispered to me with a wink.

Out of the way! Go to your classes! she sharply exclaimed, and the group, collectively moaning their disappointment, grudgingly parted.

As we passed, Martin glared at me through razor-thin eyes. Swaying like a caged animal, his chest heaved with wrathful and audible breaths. I kept my distance and my eyes on him: I had witnessed multiple fights since the beginning of the school year, and in one case a black boy punched another student while a teacher stood between them. I wasn't taking any chances.

Days later, I was told joyfully by a white-guilted girl that Martin assured his entourage he was going to beat me down when next he saw me, that I had been lucky to have had a teacher by my side, and that next time he wasn't going to let a teacher stop him from "stealing" me—the black term for sucker punching.

Chapter 25

Blighted

Seeing white girls in Martin's entourage spurred me to reflection and investigation. In conversation after conversation, class after class, week after week, I had observed white-guilt radiating most profoundly from white girls. I watched as some of the most white-guilted girls began hanging out with nonwhite boys. And I watched as some of these began dating them: Mestizos, blacks, Amerindians, Arabs, Asians, it didn't matter—so long as the boys weren't white.

When I talked with these girls, when I probed their thinking and motivations, I discovered that they were alleviating the pain of their white-guilt, that they were surrendering not only their minds, but their bodies. I noticed that they were running away from everything white: their culture, their history, their people, their families, themselves.

Why run? I wondered. And I answered myself: self-preservation by way of self-destruction. They ran and did everything they could to shed their white identity, to escape the self-hate and social condemnation of the "villain" role that the antiwhite narrative imposed on their race.

Like a disease that afflicted the thoughts, the white-guilt compelled whites to feel good about feeling bad, to derive pleasure by inducing pain, by defiling everything white—even themselves. Such

Chapter 25 *Blighted*

realizations were like coal to a boiler, spurring me to greater resolve, compelling me to take things to the next level.

Chapter 26

A Club

I knew it would be difficult to recruit members, but I had decided that the time had come to form a club to protect the wellbeing of my people and Western Civilization.

Seriously? Adam gargled, coughing and spilling Sprite on his bag of Doritos. *No way you're starting a club like that? Are you serious? You know I can't join,* he continued as though I had asked him to sacrifice babies to the Devil. *I'm not lookin' to get my teeth smashed in. And you'll definitely* (his eyes got very wide)—*you—will—definitely get suspended for starting a club that cares about white people.*

I would join, but I can't, apologized "Fearless" himself, Chris. *Everybody that joins will be kicked out of school…and every black and Mexican kid will come from miles around to beat the shit out of the members.*

Depressed, I pressed on, searching for kids like myself, kids who saw the Regime's dogma for what it was—antiwhite—and who were brave enough to take a stand against the psychological, social, and physical terrorism.

Jason, are you asking your classmates to join a white supremacist gang? indignantly hissed one of my teachers, Mrs. Ratner, pulling me aside as the class filed into the hall after the bell.

Chapter 26   *A Club*

What?! No! I'm trying to start a club for kids who don't like how whites are always portrayed as the bad guys.

That IS a white supremacist gang, Jason.

No, it's not, I disagreed, utterly confused by her frenzied effort to misrepresent MY club.

Weren't my club's purposes, intentions, definitions, and objectives mine to decide? I was starting it. Who was she to say that it was anything other than what I say it was?

I won't argue with you. You will not ask any more of your classmates to join your—she wrinkled her nose—*club.*

Two more teachers voiced similar threats the following weeks:

Do not solicit students to join any type of hate group, ordered Mrs. Elders, *uh uh, no, do not speak while I'm speaking—I don't care what you think it is...not in my classroom.*

Jason, browbeat Ms. Whitman, *I don't want you using class-time to talk about your club—it doesn't matter what Jun does. What did you say? Because Jun talking about the International Club is different. Do you really have to ask why? Because their group isn't racist*, she finished in a sharp voice.

Jason, began Mr. Wolf later in the next week, as he stopped me short in the hall, grabbing my backpack from behind, jarring and scaring me. *You're not trying to start some sort of white supremacist club here in school?*

No way. I just asked a couple kids if they'd speak out with me against how whites are always portrayed as the bad guys.

What? He closed his eyes and smiled disbelievingly, dramatically rocking his head from side to side, clearly—and ridiculously—acting as though nothing could be more absurd than claiming that white people are portrayed as bad guys.

I tried to speak, but he raised his voice in a tone of feigned concern, talking over me as a clutch of kids gathered to watch my public chastisement.

Groups like that aren't permitted. You know that. Come on…straighten up and do your schoolwork, okay? If you actually start one of those hate groups, Principal Stein will have to notify the police—and nobody wants that.

The police?! I was terrified.

Why did my teachers and the administration misrepresent my efforts? I was far too young and forthright to claim that I had ulterior motives, that I had a secret plan to conquer the school and commit atrocities against nonwhites. The only answer was that they didn't want us to come together in defense of our wellbeing—our history, heritage, interests, identity, and reputation as a people.

They claimed they wanted to prevent "white supremacism" and "hate," but I began to suspect their real worry—their secret, hidden concern—was that whites getting together to talk about our group interests might enable us to see and unify against the financial, political, physical, sexual, and emotional windfall of white-guilting us.

I was gaining a clearer picture of the world, but a voice in my head kept begging me to give up, listing and rationalizing my fears:

Chapter 26   *A Club*

beat-downs, angry teachers and administrators, suspensions, expulsion, furious and disappointed parents, police interrogations, murder. And when I finally silenced my fears, the voice argued on, listing and rationalizing my forfeited desires: good grades, friends, proud parents, popularity, girlfriends, a future.

The voice howled, growing closer and then farther, weaker and then stronger, but I kept beating it back. After my initial fear over the implication of my imprisonment (or whatever the police would do to me for starting my club), I resolved to recruit more carefully, to fly as far under the radar as possible.

Chapter 27

Claws

The bell signaling the end of class and the beginning of a six-minute period between classes had just rung. In need of a notebook, I briskly headed toward my locker. Navigating through the rambunctious crowd of book-bag-burdened students, I approached a group of black kids. Their number and exaggerated movements formed a blockade that spanned the hall from wall to wall.

Many of the blacks at my junior high were notorious for parking themselves in the path of foot traffic, being as tempestuous as possible, and daring anyone to object or to give the slightest sign of disapproval.

What you lookin' at? Why you makin' that face? You gotta problem? were typical responses when they sensed others were displeased with their behavior.

Hugging the wall, I sidled up to their lurching huddle, but just as I approached, the piercingly loud voice of a black girl delivered a cryptic punch-line.

I tol' him he not spoused to do dat!

Laughter exploded like a keg of TNT: Deafening screams, howls and hoots rang through the air. I was slammed against the wall as black kids in riotous merriment ran in every direction, gaudy adornment swinging wildly from their ears, wrists, and necks, toxic colognes coiling in their wake like invisible contrails.

Chapter 27 — *Claws*

In the blink of an eye, they had reversed course and were heedlessly running toward each other, bumping and shoving through kids as they went. But just as they began to coalesce, one of the black boys, imitating a female's voice, shouted, *That n*gga is a dumb-ass n*gga*, which caused the group to detonate again, sending blacks screaming and running in all directions as if their mythical "Klanzilla" were wading up the Potomac.

I was sick of it. I wanted them to quiet down and get the hell out of the way, so rather than squeeze by, I confidently strode through their midst as they coalesced.

Returning to the group, one of the smaller black boys heavily rammed me, inconsiderate or oblivious of my displeasure until our eyes locked for a split second. I'm certain he read exactly what was going through my mind, but he offered neither protest nor apology.

Quickly distancing myself from their rowdy barricade, I continued toward my locker. Moments later and slightly more composed, I entered the Commons, which was a popcorn-popper of activity.

I had just opened my locker door when it was fiercely kicked. The ear-splitting crash and livid shouting disoriented me, causing me to drop my books.

Nearly convulsing with fright and feeling like I was losing consciousness, I spun right and stepped backward.

An 8th grade "gangsta" Mestizo glared down at me. Boiling with rage, he stormed in my face, *Fucking gringo!*

Crucible

My mind wasn't working; I could only understand bits and pieces: shouting, angry and eager faces, a crowd of students, nonwhite boys egging on my attacker.

Kick that motha-fucka's ass!

Kick his ass! Ha ha!

The gangsta's features, twisted by volcanic rage, loomed over me as he pointed his finger in my face.

...Pussy... ...shit... motha-fucka! he hollered incoherently, his eyes flaring with scarlet veins.

Horrified, I suddenly realized I was trying to speak, but I only stuttered.

...da da da, somethin' wrong with you motha-fucka? He mockingly demanded of me to the laughter of the crowd.

I shook my head as he took hold of me, punched me in the face and flung me through the air—riding me to the floor.

A second later, I was on my belly, my left arm protecting my head and face. He was over me, to my left with his right knee on my back, throwing fisted blows that pounded my head and neck.

My thoughts were jumbled: shock—fear—pain, and then the *why* fled, the confusion dissolved, anger as a searing tempest stormed into me.

Using my right arm, I raised my body and slid my knees under me. Forcing myself upward, I reached across my chest and grabbed his shirt while he blasted my neck, ear, and the side of my face.

Chapter 27 *Claws*

Yanking with all my might while bucking upward with my pinned legs, I swung my left arm over his head as he struggled against me.

Clutching a handful of his hair, I wrenched his head backward—rose to one knee—and smashed him in the mouth with my fist.

He curled up, bringing his face to his knees. I flung myself onto him—the back of his head against my belly.

Grabbing his legs so he couldn't uncurl—I threw my knee as hard as I could, again and again, crushing him in the head and face.

Kids were screaming.

Oh shit!

Oh fuck!

Get up!

Move your head!

I was getting tired. *He'll throw me. He'll get me. I've got to do something.*

I jumped to my feet, drew back and with all my might kicked him in the ribs—the head—the face.

His skull bounced like a kickball attached to a slackening tether. He tried to get up, but his eyes rolled blearily when I kicked him in the face.

Nonwhite hands ensnared me from behind: They were clutching my clothes and throat—yanking me backward.

They were going to jump me. They were going to gang up and beat me down.

Crucible

But there were shouts, shouts that a teacher was coming. Kids ran in all directions. The gangsta's "homies" released me and disappeared, leaving me standing there in a state of shock.

Climbing to his feet and looking like a tumble-dried chupacabra—soccer shirt ripped halfway off, mussed hair, blood filling the white of his right eye and smeared across his brown face, he mumbled one last threat.

I'm gonna kill you, motha-fucka.

Chapter 27   *Claws*

Ok ok! a man's loud voice bellowed authoritatively over the heads of the scrambling kids. *Break it up! Break it up, I said! Go to your classes, or you're all getting detention.*

Adrenalin-fueled tremors and waves of heat ran through my body as I gathered my books, closed my (now-bent) locker door, and ran for my next class. When I exited the Commons, a tangible energy was still in the air, a residue of the failed attempt by antiwhites to bludgeon the heresy out of me, a "progressive," "liberal" act presided over by one observer who hadn't fled: stern, silent, leering—the Idol.

Chapter 28

Poisoned Faith

Even though I had won the fight ("narrowly" won the fight by fighting "dirty," as the account spread itself around the school) and even though I was happy that I could take a punch and fight back, I was humiliated by the way I had stuttered in front of everyone.

I wanted revenge. I wanted to surprise my attacker as he had surprised me, hit him without warning as he had hit me without warning, make him pay for humiliating me. But I was afraid, and I was opposed to jumping him because I had been taught that such behavior was wrong—and more specifically, unbecoming of a Christian.

While I had considered myself a Christian since my earliest years at Christian preschool, I had only begun regularly attending church the previous year. Accompanying friends and their families, I made a circuit of different Christian denominations. Though each denomination had slightly different teachings, all preached and praised passivity as the means by which to deal with an enemy. So I swallowed my pride and quenched my anger.

But I was conflicted. I was beginning to question the teachings of Christianity: Antiwhitism's version of history and codes of right and wrong were adopted as Christian law at every church I attended, and where there was conflict between the Bible and antiwhite doctrine, antiwhite doctrine always trumped the Bible.

Chapter 28 *Poisoned Faith*

The book of books, which they said was the word of God, was regularly and slyly adapted to antiwhitism, effeminately interpreted through the lens of antiwhitism, and applied only in so far as permitted by antiwhitism. I was getting the same antiwhite doctrine at church that I received in school and from the media. There was simply no escaping it.

I wasn't ready to turn my back on the Church, but every time Christianity conflicted with the dignity, identity, and wellbeing of my people, I deemed it wrong, and when it advanced antiwhite dictates as the word of God—I despised it.

Chapter 29

Imposters

W*ggers: They were one of the oddest spectacles at my junior high. Many of the kids were mystified by the sudden appearance of these pretenders.

Why in hell do they dress and act like that? kids would ask, pulling the sort of face that one wears when viewing a Rorschach test.

The blacks make fun of them, they would astutely observe.

Everyone thinks they're a joke for trying to be what they're not, they would opine.

Are they retarded? they would ask, and invariably the consensus was—*yes!*

To play the role of an inner-city black thug, *w*ggers* had to act as though they were as dimwittedly vicious as inner-city black thugs. But there was more to their role-playing than appearances; they knew they were a joke, and as a result, some were genuinely violent: It must not have been easy to be a *w*gger* and dread the snigger, to be mocked when you're LARPing a "badass."

I probed *w*ggers* for their motivations. I watched their transformations from normal white kids to role-players. It didn't take long to figure out what caused their conversions.

The schools and entertainment media taught us that all the races were the same—except that nonwhites were better dancers, better lovers, and better athletes—that they were wiser, smarter, and friendlier. We were taught that there were no differences among the races except that nonwhites were more spiritual, more family oriented, and more in touch with nature—that they were hipper, happier, and kinder. We were taught that there was only one human race, but that nonwhites were more understanding, more sensitive, and more helpful—that they were stronger, sadder, and brighter. We were told that they were harder working, more faithful, more in touch with God and the universe, more adept at solving problems, more able to feel and understand the pain of others, more likely to come to the aid of the underdog, and we were threatened with the specter that to think otherwise was to be labeled racist.

We were also taught by the entertainment media that everything black was better and cooler than everything else: blacks were cooler, their bodies were cooler, their clothes were cooler, their music, cars, names, and lives were cooler. And conversely, everything white was uncool, pathetic, puny, feeble, impotent, backward, and unathletic: our bodies, our minds, our skin, our ideas, our clothes, our music, everything.

The schools and entertainment media taught us that all the races were the same, except that the white race was uniquely villainous, prone to greed, and fundamentally immoral—that whites were likely to destroy the cultures of others, likely to exploit others, and likely to ethnically cleanse others. We were taught that there were no differences between the races, except that the white race had no culture, no positive identity, and no commendable history—that whites were not a people, not a race, and not a community. We were

Crucible

taught that there was only one human race, but that whites were uniquely disposed to being bigoted, racist, homophobic, xenophobic, and anti-Semitic.

Consequently—and INFINITELY unsurprisingly—all of my white peers clung to identities other than white: They had nonwhite ancestors, or they identified with nonwhites, or they imitated nonwhites, or they adopted nonwhite cultures, or they were antiwhite, or they were "skaters," or "metalheads," or "Christians," or whatever—so long as they weren't white. This was the first driver behind the appearance of *w*ggers*.

White was uncool, flaccid, and wicked, while black was cool, robust, and desirable. And this context, coupled with the new desire for female attention, formed the second driver behind the appearance of *w*ggers*. To get female attention, some white boys aped the "cooler" blacks, and the gimmick often worked, because it wasn't just the white boys who had been taught that white was uncool, flaccid, and wicked, while black was cool, robust, and desirable—but the white girls as well.

Chapter 30

Beyond the Walls

No one would walk home with me after school, which hurt my feelings, but also gave me time to think, to reflect on my situation and all the mechanisms and motivations that worked to the detriment of my people.

Today was no different than any other. I trudged down the sidewalk, studying two *w*ggers* from my school. Limping along on the other side of the street, their pants hanging low on their hips, I wondered how they reconciled their white skin with their new persona, but my thoughts leapt to an eerie sensation crawling over the back of my neck like a black centipede.

Turning, I saw three 7th or 8th grade black boys about twenty yards behind me, one of whom I thought I recognized from school. They sped up as soon as I spotted them.

Who are they? I asked myself, shooting another quick glance over my shoulder and stepping up my pace. *It's probably nothing. They're probably just hurrying somewhere.*

But there was something about the way they looked at me—something in their eyes. They didn't seem uninterested. They weren't preoccupied; they were intent—but intent on what?

I glanced back. They sped up.

I started walking even faster, noticing the *w*ggers* keenly watching the black kids gaining on me.

Hold up! one of the black boys shouted, the three quickening their pace as I threw another frightened look over my shoulder.

Wait a minute! another one bellowed, their strides breaking into intermittent skips.

Hang on! one called after me, an artificial note of pleasantness to his voice. *We juss wanna aks you som'fin!*

Are they serious? Should I stop? Do I look stupid for being scared?

At that moment, a memory hit me with a jolt that tore through my frame like thunder: A black cousin from juvie had promised to kill me on my way home from school.

It's him! my thoughts desperately screamed, cold sweat and shudders crawling through my skin. *Oh my god!*

Electricity pulsing through my body, I unconsciously started to jog, and that's when they began to sprint.

A moment later and I was running for my life, putting more and more distance between us.

I'm'a kill you, white boy!
White motha-fucka—pussy!
We gonna get you, cracker!

They chased me for two blocks before giving up, but I wouldn't be so lucky in the weeks to come.

Chapter 31

By Terror, They Rule

I had hoped my successes on the basketball court and baseball field would increase my likeability and make it easier to recruit members to my club, but unlike my accomplishments on the football field, basketball and baseball did little for my reputation. But even if they had, I'm not sure it would have helped. Most kids refused to share their feelings on the wellbeing of our people and how we were treated, clearly afraid of the consequences of deviating from antiwhitism. Those who were willing to give their opinions would only do so in secret.

I probed my peers' hearts for defiance, but there was none. I looked for the determination and strength to resist, but those qualities were missing. I searched for pride, faith, and confidence, but these, too, were absent. I would have said they were empty if it were not for the abject hopelessness that pervaded their hearts. They shouldn't have known such secret despair.

From their deepest core, where they hid their darkest pain from the world, they revealed how they felt about themselves and our people.

We didn't do anything, but we're blamed for everything, they lamented.

Why aren't we allowed to be proud? The minorities are encouraged to be proud.

It's really unfair but there's nothing we can do about it.
Why won't anyone help us?
Why do we have to make up for things we didn't do?
There's no future for us.
Why are we punished for being white?
Why is it okay to discriminate against us?
They can do anything they want to us and it's okay.
Why is it evil to care about our people?
They hate us, the entire system hates us—we might as well kill ourselves.

Despite the endless antiwhite education and entertainment, I discovered that by encouraging my peers to talk about such things, by encouraging them to investigate their feelings, ask questions, and focus on subjects the Regime declared off limits and punishable, many of them secretly agreed with me. They were merely confused, browbeaten, shamed, despondent, terrorized, silenced—abused.

Why won't they help me? I desperately asked myself. *If we'd all just stand together…if we'd all just stand up and in one voice say—ENOUGH!*

But I didn't know how to convince them to stand. I could offer them self-respect, pride, a healthy identity, but our antiwhite victimizers would ruin them: They would smear, ostracize, and physically attack them. A healthy identity and a promise of its benefits were not enough when weighed against antiwhite terrorism.

I didn't give up on inspiring others, but I gave up on starting a club. I simply had no answers. And more importantly, summer

Chapter 31   *By Terror, They Rule*

vacation was on its way: Another month of school and I would be free—no more fear of beat-downs, no more antiwhite lessons, no more white girls snubbing me because I wasn't antiwhite.

Chapter 32

Heartache

The week's final bell had unleashed the chaos of a stick-prodded anthill; students, parents, teachers, busses, and cars hurried in all directions. I had planted myself on a strip of warm grass beside the school, waiting for Chris and Adam: Mr. Cribbs was questioning them about a fight they had seen earlier in the day.

The sting of being a social outcast hit me in waves as I watched pairs and groups of kids frolic by, ignoring me as though I were just another blade of grass. Mercifully, the crossing guard's whistle diverted my attention.

As I watched the busses roll out of the school's lot like a long, segmented, yellow snake, I noticed Mrs. Peyton strolling to her car.

Bye, Mrs. Peyton, I called out to her, waving my hand over my head.

Jason, she chimed, changing course and walking over, her heels clicking on the pavement and her keys musically dangling from her finger. *It's Friday; why aren't you headed home like everyone else?*

I'm waiting for Adam and Chris, I said over the chirping of two male cardinals battling among the branches of a linden.

What I didn't reveal was that I was waiting for them because they had talked to Fox about me.

Are you three doing something this evening?

Chapter 32   Heartache

Yeah, I fibbed, not wanting her pity.

I'm glad. Well, have a nice weekend, she lilted, turning gracefully on her heel with a little wave and heading to her car.

I turned my attention to the squabbling birds. I wondered what they were fighting over until I noticed a female cardinal watching the combat from a perch in a crape myrtle. As I focused on her keen eyes and sharp crest, the blurred image of Adam and Chris loping over from the school appeared in the distance beyond her.

Hey, what happened with Cribbs?

Not much, said Chris, twisting the corner of his lips indifferently. *He just wanted to know how the kid got his head split open.*

God! Did he bleed a lot? I queasily asked, rising and stretching my legs.

Oh yeah, croaked Adam as Chris, wide-eyed, nodded vigorously.

So what did you guys find out about Fox? I blurted, despite trying to play it cool.

A busted head and profuse bleeding was morbidly captivating, but I desperately needed to know what Fox had said. There were only a few weeks left in the school year to get her to like me.

Adam studied my shoes and Chris looked at me from under his brow.

What? What is it? I anxiously asked the two of them.

Crucible

Dread swirled around me. *She doesn't like me*, I hastily thought. *It's because I care about our people....*

Well—she—don't worry about her, said Adam delicately, raising his eyes and sympathetically tilting his head.

What do you mean, 'don't worry about her?'

I just...she's not—worth your time, Adam fumbled.

What are you saying? What did she say to you guys? I asked, fear skipping on blocks of ice up my back.

She doesn't like you, said Chris flatly.

Yeah but screw her, said Adam emphatically.

I know...but Jason needed to know what she said.

A cold stillness enveloped me, and then something began rushing through my insides, falling toward emptiness, seemingly taking the sun and all happiness with it. I didn't want to know any more, but I heard myself ask in a small, hollow voice, *Why doesn't she like me?*

Adam and Chris exchanged nervous looks before Chris spoke up.

She said that you say a lot of racist things, and that she would never like a racist.

Is that really what she said? I asked, looking weakly at Adam for confirmation.

He nodded reluctantly.

All right...well, that's that, I guess. I'll see you guys on Monday, I mumbled, shielding my face and briskly heading home.

Chapter 32 *Heartache*

    I had revealed a lot to Adam and Chris: my fears about being beaten-down, my grief over the loss of my friends, my sorrow over my rejection by the girls, my hope that Fox would like me, but I didn't want them to see the sadness washing over my face.

Chapter 33

Caught

Even though Adam, Chris, and I had planned to meet at Adam's house right after school to discuss our summer plans, I had stayed late with Mrs. Swan to complete a paper. Thirty minutes later, I set off for Adam's under a clear, warm sky with nothing but my book-bag and thoughts.

I trooped along a chain-link fence over a set of manicured softball and soccer fields on the school's back lot. Lost in a daydream about summer's freedom and counting the dandelions along the fence's base, I didn't notice the two black boys approaching until they were right beside me.

Where you gonna run now, motha-fucka? jeered one into my silence, black as his Oakland Raiders t-shirt, his features haughty and wrathful.

It's him! He's the one, my thoughts stammered. *The one who promised to kill me!*

There was nowhere to run. I was boxed in. The world leapt into poignant vividness as though a camera lens had been screwed into focus.

He and his friend, wearing Adidas high tops and eyeing me with a sharp, angry glare, were the unfamiliar boys who had chased me weeks earlier.

Chapter 33   *Caught*

What do you want? I blurted in a blank tone as Adidas circled to my left, a noisy car rumbling beyond a hedge of pine trees behind the fence.

You gotta problem wit my peoples, motha-fucka?! growled Oakland, stepping forward and throwing his arms wide—head height.

I had seen the trick before. Black kids at my school used it all the time. They would get their victim talking, draw within inches, hands out to their sides, palms forward, and then without warning— make a fist and *steal* their victim in the face.

I jumped backward along the fence, my clothes and book-bag snagging on its wire-ties, their bitter points gouging my skin, stinging hot and raw through my fear.

Adidas leapt to his right and crouched like he was about to tackle me.

Where you goin', motha-fucka? demanded Oakland, taking a large, menacing stride toward me.

I threw my book-bag at his face.

Leave me alone!

Swatting it to the ground, he kicked it off to the side and turned back to me with a face like murder.

What had I done?

Awww dat's it, motha-fucka! You gonna get it! he roared, making tight circles with his fists by his chest, thumbs sticking out like a hitchhiker.

Crucible

I had never thrown punches like a boxer. I didn't know what to do, and though Adidas hadn't balled his fists, I knew he'd jump in: The nonwhites almost always jumped in.

Standing lefthanded so I could face Adidas, I raised my fists—just in time—as Oakland launched himself at me. Swinging madly, his roundhouse punches hurdled by my head, grazing and bouncing off my face.

Our arms tangled wildly as he threw on me and I blocked and shoved him.

Jump the fence, shouted a voice in my head. *They'll get me before I'm over it*, a thought shouted back.

He came again, swatting my hands with his left and throwing his right. His punch grazed my forehead.

Adidas angled to throw a punch, but Oakland was on me. I leaned in and shoved him backward. He lost and regained his footing. We squared off, our fists raised.

My eyes on Adidas, Oakland rushed in with a kick to my groin, but he missed, striking my inner thigh and retreating, his fists in tight circles by his face.

Fiery pain shot up and down my inner leg: *Is the muscle torn?!*

Blazing with hatred, eyes narrowed, Oakland ran forward—throwing wild rights—I shoved him—he stumbled—I stepped forward—he fought to regain his balance—and I kicked him *hard* and square between the legs!

Oh fuck! yelled Adidas, his eyes gaping, staring searchingly at Oakland.

Chapter 33   *Caught*

Naww, fuck dat, Oakland snarled dismissively, cinching up and then digging at the top of his jeans. *It ain't na'fin.*

A tense moment waxed as Oakland seemed to be trying to decide if he wanted to continue, but as the seconds ticked, I noticed the fight leaving his face—panic taking its place.

Fuck dis shit, he spat, a note of feigned courage thinly covering the warble of pain in his voice.

He dropped his fists and edged to my left before collapsing.

Adidas was shouting and Oakland was moaning like a maimed animal. I grabbed my book-bag and ran.

I sprinted for a mile before I started to tire. Too amped and too frightened to be anywhere but home, I took a winding route through multiple neighborhoods, walking for nearly two hours: sneaking, hiding, nursing my wounds, fearfully scanning for the predators who stalked me, for the endlessly self-proclaimed "victimized" banner-bearers of "social justice."

Chapter 34

Surrender

I was summoned to the office the following Monday. Once there, one of the secretaries tonelessly informed me that Mr. Cribbs wanted to speak with me. As I bewilderedly approached his lamplit, coconut-scented office, I heard Cribbs and Wolf gabbing amiably, but they went stoically silent the moment I entered: Cribbs behind his desk, Wolf seated in an adjacent chair, wielding a multipage document that he rolled-up as I entered the room.

Mr. Köhne, said Cribbs, unsmiling.

Take a seat, Jason, added Wolf flatly, pointing with the rolled-up document at the empty chair by the end table and box of tissues.

I had never seen Cribbs or Wolf so troubled.

What's wrong? What's happened? Is my family okay? a voice desperately cried in my head, as I threw anxious looks at the pair and perched myself on the edge of my seat. *Hurry up! What's wrong!*

Jason, Cribbs thoughtfully began, leaning forward and resting his elbows on his desk, lacing his fingers, *we're concerned about your bullying behavior.*

My what?! I choked incredulously, gaping at them both.

I couldn't believe what I was hearing: What bullying behavior? I had barely survived a year of being excoriated, snubbed, abandoned, silenced, chased, intimidated, threatened with beat-downs

Chapter 34 — Surrender

and murder, and physically attacked, and they wanted to talk about *MY* bullying behavior?

Your bullying—yes, Cribbs adamantly continued despite the look of disbelieving shock on my face. *We're concerned because you've been intolerant of others' views all year.*

*No, that's not—*I energetically started, but Cribbs showed me the palm of his hand, silencing me.

Don't you think you've been a little insensitive to others this year? asked Cribbs, lifting his brow and nodding—encouraging me to agree.

No, I shot briskly, feeling as though hyenas were circling out of the office's dark corners.

This is a serious matter, Jason, he continued in a sterner air, shifting his coffee cup from one side of his desk to the other, following it with his eyes as he spoke. *You've intimidated and frightened other students with your views. Now—I'm sure that's not what you wanted.... Oh* (he paused, fixing me with a knowing glare) *and we know about your fights with students who disagreed with you.*

They came after me! I countered, sliding back in my seat, feeling scared, confused, and defensive.

You've incited them with the things you've said, interrupted Wolf moralistically, tapping my knee with the rolled-up document. *We've talked about this several times. I know—no, I know what you're about to say, but people are naturally defensive when they hear opinions like those.*

Defensive?! I exclaimed.

Crucible

This couldn't be happening. They couldn't really be accusing me of everything the antiwhites were guilty of. They couldn't be turning reality on its head, making the antiwhites into victims—and me into the victimizer...but they were! I felt myself shrinking, the air leaving my lungs beneath the horrible weight of my epiphany.

Hearing the views that led to so much suffering is (he looked to the ceiling, searching for the right words)...*it's like experiencing the fear and oppression of slavery or the Holocaust,* said Wolf in a voice both mournful and righteous. *Don't you understand? It's hurtful.*

Views that led to so much suffering? Hurtful? What was he talking about?! All I had wanted was dignity for my people: no more white-guilting us, no more portraying us as the bad guys, no more preventing us from having our own identity, no more demonizing us for having pride in who we are and all that we've accomplished.

Your classmates can't speak freely because they're afraid of what you might say, added Cribbs pointedly, shaking his head reproachfully as though I—rather than they—were responsible for speech codes. *Jason, do you have any idea what it's like to be afraid to share your thoughts?*

I do, I jumped in, nodding and ready to defend myself before Wolf silenced me, disappointedly frowning.

That's ridiculous, roared Cribbs exasperatedly. *You've no idea what it's like to be around someone who holds oppressive views. Listen to me, young man, though youuu might not be hateful, a lot of the things you say represent hate...and intolerance, for that matter,*

Chapter 34 *Surrender*

and there's no place for those things in modern America. Besides, you want to be liked by your classmates, don't you? You just have to put this stuff to bed, he finished, taking a deep breath and throwing a restless glance at Wolf.

Firmly patting my knee again with the rolled-up document, Wolf said, *Jason, we don't want this to be a problem next year.*

But I've only been asking for dignity for my people, I whimpered despairingly, sensing that nothing I could say would change their minds.

Cribbs rolled his eyes, shook his head and chuckled to himself as he moved his coffee cup back to the other side of his desk.

Jason. Please. That isn't productive. Can we count on you to put all this behind us so it isn't a problem next year? continued Wolf in a tone that conveyed authority and inflexibility.

How could I say no? How could I say no as two of the highest powers in the school—two of the highest powers in my world—held my head under water?

I had been abandoned by friends, spurned by white girls, bullied by teachers, betrayed by my people, threatened, stalked, and attacked by nonwhites, cast to the wolves by the administration, and now, history had been rewritten by the authorities—the roles of its players reversed.

Sitting there—the only white child in the school who hadn't surrendered—listening to adults invert reality, refusing to hear my plea, refusing to be fair, my thoughts winged their way from my body. They sped from the office, out to the hall that joined the building's

Crucible

front doors, past the cafeteria, beyond the trophy case, into the Commons and over the lockers.... There, with my mind's eye, I bitterly looked upon the Idol—and then, I too, surrendered.

Chapter 35

Darkness

Cribbs and Wolf had demanded that I change my behavior, that I stop speaking out against, stop undermining, stop illustrating the double standards of their antiwhite dogma, but my behavior, my stance, my ideological endurance had not been a whim—it had been an expression of my spirit.

Under the pretext of instilling tolerance and equality, they demanded intolerance and inequality. They demanded a fanatical repudiation of everything that obstructed their antiwhite objectives. And like crazed preachers, frothing with religious fervor, they exorcised disagreement.

The freedom of summer and the joy of its promise had finally arrived—but not for me. The bliss of carefree afternoons and the tart kiss of lemonade beckoned the thirsty—but I heard no summons. The felicity of sunshine-washed days and firefly-dappled nights wrapped around its revelers—but I wasn't one of them.

The shutters closed and the door barred, my head drooping heavily over my lap, I brooded while the voices of summer sang beyond my bedroom window. I couldn't stop thinking about Cribbs and Wolf; the previous school year; the way I had been treated by my peers, teachers, and the administration; and how I was going to reconcile an antiwhite persona with a spirit that loathed injustice and lived for the glory of the West.

Crucible

As I gloomily reflected on my experiences, I realized, with the explosive abruptness of a starting pistol, that everything I had feared about the dogma that dominated the West was true: It had named an enemy which its purpose was to fight—an enemy to unify and motivate its followers—a scapegoat to blame for the dogma's and its followers' weaknesses and failings—a menace that fueled the dogma's continued existence and justified its demands for blind obedience, faith, and violence. And I realized, with my mouth agape, that the group the dogma had named "enemy" was *my people*.

Lifting my eyes and staring blankly into the darkness, I laughed bitterly. I had refused to believe my gut. I had argued with myself, forcing myself to give those whom I ignorantly called by the names of their taking ("liberal," "progressive," etc.) the benefit of the doubt: *They were honestly trying to help others. They were inadvertently harming my people in the process. All I had to do was make them aware of their error.*

With the galvanizing surge and white flash of insight that follows realization, I finally understood that there was no misunderstanding.

I clicked on an anemic lamp that hung from my bedpost, and I paced the shadow-strewn floor. The antiwhites were not honest people inadvertently harming whites in an effort to help others—NO!—they were using the *excuse* of helping others to dispossess, disinherit, and displace my people.

The so-called "threat" of "white supremacism" was a bogey they used to white-guilt and intimidate us to prevent us from coming together in defense of our wellbeing, a unity that would eventually deprive them of the financial, political, physical, sexual, and emotional windfall of white-guilting us.

JEALOUSLY—ENVY—HATRED—GREED—LUST—HUBRIS—BASELESS REVENGE—SELF-RIGHTEOUSNESS—MEGALOMANIA—SADISM...these were their motivations!

They're profiteers, I thought to myself, shivering with the horrible truth of their hungers. *They're profiting from the harm they do to us!*

I raised the slats of my shutters just enough to peer out onto the now-quiet street.

Freed of my blinders, a thought burst into my mind: They had enshrined their carnal hungers in the body of a secular religion. And they had used the mountaintops of the news and entertainment media and educational systems to preach, proselytize, and propagate their antiwhite religion.

I lowered my eyes and closed the shutters, my mind afire with the realization that they practiced their antiwhite religion as though it had been penned by God rather than jealous men and women, as though any act that served its ends was justified. Like a statue cut to a pensive mood, I stood in the center of my room with the weight of my epiphany crushing me.

I had no idea from what dank hole this putrid, antiwhite ideology and the afterbirth of its proponents had crawled, but I knew—despite its endless claims that it was the underdog, the voice of freedom fighting against an oppressor—I knew that *IT* was the oppressor, that *IT* dominated the news and entertainment media, that *IT* dominated the political and educational discourse, that *IT* was the establishment.

Clicking off the light, I collapsed onto my bed, a sea of hopelessness suddenly washing over me.

I knew, then, that I would have to deny my people for my whole life: I would have to religiously practice antiwhitism if I wanted to be accepted, if I wanted to receive good grades, if I wanted to get a good job and be awarded promotions, if I wanted the love of a white woman. I knew that I would have to be antiwhite or disparaged—antiwhite or hated.

I was trapped: too fearful and hopeless to soldier on for my people, and yet too devoted to my people to surrender my identity.

As I stared unfocusedly into the darkened silence of my bedroom, emotions like dark clouds bathed my will in arctic rains—and yet, somehow, even as I drifted into a restless sleep, even as apathy's slurry-iced waters restlessly crept into every fiber of my being, a quenchless fire burned within me.

Chapter 36

Starlight

An odd desire compelled me to dig aimlessly through the books and loose papers on my parents' bookshelves the following morning. While fingering through yellowing documents, I chanced upon the military paperwork of a relative I didn't know I had, a cavalryman in the Army of Northern Virginia, Confederate States of America.

Old copies of the original documents, they had been used by one of my great aunts to prove her relation to a soldier of the South when she joined the Daughters of the Confederacy. My eyes followed the gentle cursive lines of a steady hand across the timeworn pages. That soldier, my kin, had flown to the defense of his country at the start of the war.

He left behind a simple home and a wife and children as he rode off to an uncertain fate. I had no doubt he was afraid of what might befall his family in his absence, frightened by the prospect of being maimed, scared he might never return to his loved ones. And I had no doubt that, despite these and other concerns, he did what our people have always done: He mustered his courage and daring—and he went forth to glory.

The voices of his wife and children, I was equally certain, mournfully echoed in his ears as he trod the lonely roads of war.

You come back to us, his loving wife likely urged through stoic tears, a strong façade for the sake of the children. *Don't you leave us alone.*

His children doubtlessly threw their little arms around his neck as they clung fast to the moments before goodbye.

Don't go! they likely sobbed. *We love you, daddy.*

Kneeling at the base of my parents' bookshelf, holding the documents that chronicled my ancestor's enlistment and his death on the battlefield three and a half years later, a voice spoke amid my tears, summoning me to duty as my ancestors had been summoned, urging me to fight back.

Driven by a spirit beyond my control, I feverishly scoured my parents' garage, digging, shifting, searching for a Confederate flag I knew was tucked away somewhere in the clutter. A souvenir from a "Civil War" reenactment (the only reenactment to which my parents had taken us years earlier), the flag had spoken to me with an unrivaled power and beauty.

And there it was—there—as I moved some old, dust-covered auto-mechanic magazines, I caught sight of a single shining star amid the clutter. Time slowed. It wasn't just an eighteen by twelve-inch cotton flag that stared back at me: it was the spirit of resistance, the symbol of freedom, the will to victory.

I froze, smitten by discovery as though thunder and bolt had riven my core. The voice that had spoken to me, propelling me again and again against the awesome might of the enemy, revealed itself to

Chapter 36   *Starlight*

me at last: older than the ancient gods, loftier than the new, power that required no faith—it was the Spirit of the West.

I slowly pawed at the remaining clutter as one who carefully raises treasure or exhumes a holy relic from its hollow. As I unfolded the flag and set my eyes upon its power and beauty, a resolve hardened within me: The antiwhites in the news and entertainment media, the schools, the books, the streets, they weren't misguided "bleeding hearts" or unbiased "do-gooders," they were the enemy, and from that moment forward—I would take the fight to them!

Chapter 37

Preparation

Taking my defiance to the next level was going to be dangerous. I would attract the attention and hatred of every antiwhite in the school. The social lynching, antiwhite tribunals, and violence they had already subjected me to would pale in comparison. I would be alone again. No one would stand with me or watch my back. And worse, I feared that the *monster* Adam had half-seriously warned me about, the one who would embody antiwhite hate and bloodlust, could still be out there, fate drawing our paths together like threads on a loom. I had to prepare.

Though I was strong for my size and age group, I didn't feel I was strong enough to properly defend myself. To the regimen of sit-ups and pushups I did with my father, I added pull-ups, chin-ups, and squat thrusts.

Eager to see me excel in sports, my father had built an exercise machine, on which I did bench and shoulder press as well as squats and curls. Modeled on the Soloflex, my father had made several ingenious additions, including a speed bag that I mastered and burned off its hinges.

Knowing I would need to punch my attackers, I experimented with different ways of holding my fists and delivering punches, seeking to make the most of leverage and thereby deliver the most concentrated and devastating force: using my hips and rotating on the

Chapter 37 *Preparation*

balls of my feet like swinging a baseball bat, angling and throwing my strikes like stiff-arming in football.

But knowing how to strike wasn't enough; I needed to know where to strike. For several days I probed my face, neck, ribs, and belly for weak spots, places I knew I had to protect. During one of these exercises, I discovered a spot on my face I termed the "knockout zone." I was confident that I could disable or even knockout my attackers by blasting that spot.

With the same dedication, attention to detail, and perseverance I applied to my athletics, I prepared myself mentally, training my muscle memory, imagining myself being attacked, taking and throwing punches, moving and grappling with attackers. And going a step further, I shadowboxed in front of a mirror, keeping my fists in front of my face, my elbows tucked in, sliding, weaving, striking.

I didn't know whether or not I would defeat my attackers, but as I prepared for the *conformists* to physically punish me for my nonconformity, I swore upon everything I held dear that I would make them pay a terrible price.

Chapter 38

New Rules

While practicing long-toss baseball against the elementary school's windowless rear wall, I heard a boy's distant voice trudge through the languid heat-waves rising from the sizzling blacktop: *Hey! Heyyy! JAAASAAHHHN!*

Turning, I spotted Craig, a boy who lived nearby, but in a different school district. He and Andre, a black kid I knew from playing pickup basketball a few times at local courts, ambled over: Andre dribbling a basketball back and forth between his legs, Craig wiping sweat from his brow with the back of his hand.

You guys up to no good? I panted, throwing and then fielding the returning baseball as they took seats on the playground equipment behind me.

We talked about sports under Washington's humid, summer air, which like a hot gel, unmercifully pressed in upon us. When the conversation turned to girls, Andre complained about the white girls who wouldn't *get with him*.

Mmm hmm, he nodded, casting a knowing, sidelong glance at us as he spun his basketball wobblingly atop his finger, *you know they prejudice*.

Anger surged like geysers through me, causing fresh beads of sweat to jump from my skin.

Chapter 38   *New Rules*

He's guilting white girls into having sex with him, I thought to myself, *and when they refuse, he calls them racists.*

In the past, I would've had a furious internal debate: ignore what he had said and change the subject, or politely disagree before changing the subject. But now—now, I was different.

Are you seriously saying they're racists just because they won't open their legs for you? I accusingly shot back at him, my thoughts instinctively jumping to the Confederate flag I had taken to carrying in my pocket everywhere I went.

Yeah! Shit! he barked, fleetly snatching the basketball from midair as Craig tried to apologize for the white girls' behavior. *And even when they wanna get on it, they parents won't let 'em.*

That's their preference, jackass—there's nothing wrong with that, I argued, despite the fact that Andre was older, athletic, and taller than me.

He menacingly rose from his perch, tossed his basketball to Craig, and stepped toward me.

He obviously expected me to react like Craig: apologetic, deferential, sympathetic, guilty.

You got a problem? You racist? We didn't want to be up in this shit, he angrily blustered, contemptuously scowling as though he was affronted by a member of an inferior class.

What do you mean "this shit?" America? If whites are so evil and you're so damned oppressed, why don't you get the fuck out?!

Fuck you, white bread!

I know why you stay, jackass. You're after the white girls...not to mention every single thing that we invent and build!

My people built this country, bitch! he righteously exclaimed, as though I were a guest or trespasser on the land of his fathers.

Oh, really? This country was ninety percent white until the 1960s, right. The remainder were blacks, Asians, Mestizos, Indians...so don't give me that bullshit that ten percent of the population did all the work! Besides, if your people built America, they would have built Americas everywhere they live on the planet— and they haven't, but my people have!

Chapter 38 *New Rules*

Fuck you! How long you gonna be here?! he demanded, the ghost of a malevolent thought sweeping across his scowling face.

Oh, I see! You're gonna get your homies because you can't fight me on your own? I growled, throwing my baseball glove to the ground as though it was a gauntlet, and feeling—like it had its own heartbeat—my rebel flag in my pocket.

I could bust your block!

His eyes revealed a hint of uncertainty, but he stepped forward with his hands out in the air, clearly hoping I would cave or let him get close enough to *steal me* while we argued—so I leapt forward, my defense in my fist, and I blasted him in the face!

Like wet laundry falling from a clothesline, Andre crumpled to the ground, unmoving and unconscious.

Holy fuck, breathed Craig as he staggered backward in shock, dropping the basketball, his wide gaze bouncing between the antiwhite and his victim-turned-conqueror.

I was briefly shocked, myself. The blow sounded like a melon being kicked apart, and with a sudden rush of horror, I thought Andre dead until I noticed him breathing.

Minutes later, it was all over. The fight was behind me as I walked home with my bucket of baseballs and glove. Though I felt bad about hurting Andre, I didn't feel the need to vomit after the fight. I was different—I had changed.

Chapter 39

Identities

The antiwhites lied when they blustered that serving the Spirit of the West was an expression of hatred for nonwhites. I had submitted myself to the service of the West, and yet my friendships with nonwhites hadn't changed. They knew they could never be antiwhite around me, that I was unlike other whites—apologetic, deferential, self-effacing. They knew I didn't suffer from white-guilt and its crippling symptoms, that I wouldn't tolerate antiwhite remarks.

And I never objected to their racial identities, which were central to their lives. They talked about *their* people, *their* customs, *their* culture, *their* burgeoning influence and power. They talked about their ethnic networking and how it benefited their elders (and would benefit them in their futures) in admissions, business deals, job-placement, and career advancement. They talked about how their peoples were moving into this or that sector of the economy—proudly declaring their growing dominance.

When the lawful nonwhite kids talked about getting rich off the *stupid public*, and when the unlawfully-disposed nonwhite kids talked about schemes to steal or sell drugs, they all excluded their own peoples from victimization. They saw themselves as groups with group interests, identities, and enemies.

They spoke of their peoples as though they were creeping vines in an unsuspecting forest, growing and climbing, growing and

Chapter 39   *Identities*

webbing, growing and crowding out the other plants, taking the light of the sun for themselves. It was revelatory—insidious—frightening.

They were as racially devoted to their peoples as whites lacked any sense of racial devotion, as concerned with advancing the interests of their groups as whites lacked any concern whatsoever for the interests of our group. And yet it was whites who were damned for scheming for white dominance, whites who were damned for practicing ethnic networking, whites who were damned for profiting from being white.

The gulf between reality and the Antiwhite Narrative was colossal.

Chapter 40

Targeted

I have to share my room with my sister! dramatically exclaimed Haroon, a saucer-eyed friend, shaking his head and characteristically turning to the clear sky over his parents' driveway, as though beseeching the Lord for deliverance.

What for? I asked from my knees without lifting my gaze, my fingers covered in black grease, struggling to fit my bike's chain back over its sprocket.

My dad got a government job for a guy from my country. He's gonna stay with us for a couple months.

He's not related to you?

Nope. My dad's cousin knows him.... Oh wait! he gave a start, *I heard you knocked out a kid?!*

Yeah, I did—

You know Reggie—Haroon's eyes got even wider—*Reggie...the black kid who's gonna be a freshman this coming year? Lives over past Maynard Hill. He said he wants to fight you for that.*

Fight me for what? For knocking out Andre? I said indignantly, letting the bike-chain fall limply to the ground. *Does he even know Andre?*

Nope—said he doesn't. I asked. What happened in the fight?

Chapter 40 *Targeted*

Hold on. I pleaded, wanting him to slow down, my mind spinning. *So he wants to fight me because I won—and I'm white and Andre's black?*

Obviously, he responded briskly with a look that said my question was idiotic. *You know how that goes.*

I was furious. The antiwhites had been sending unanswered messages for far too long. It was time someone sent a message back.

I rose determinedly.

You gonna see him soon—Reggie? All right.... Tell him to bring it. Tell him I'll be at the tennis courts over by the battlefield on Sunday...at 1:00. And tell him that since he wants to gang up on the white guy, I'm not only gonna knock him out; I'm gonna stomp him into the ground.

Chapter 41

Church Friend

I grabbed a seat behind a pretty, red-headed 10th grader as our Wednesday-night Bible study instructor, a throwback to 60s era hippie culture, shuffled through the door. I tilted toward Daren, a bi-racial (white and black) friend of mine, and told him that I wouldn't be at church the following Sunday.

Damn! I wish I could be there! he bellowed jealously. *Why can't you fight 'im when I can watch?*

Daren was a good friend. His mother (a white woman) and her live-in boyfriend (an Amerindian Mexican named Miguel) ferried me to and from church twice a week. I went with them on overnight trips and to picnics organized by the church, and we even had complementary roles in a church play. But not everyone in Daren's family was as friendly as Daren.

Miguel's two sons hated me. Both were younger than me and Daren. The older of the two, one year younger than me, would mock me—in terrible English—for not being able to speak Spanish. He and his brother would glare at me. He told me that nobody wanted me there, and he would taunt me threateningly in Spanish.

I wanted to answer his taunts. I wanted to ask if he liked *my* country. I wanted to tell him to head for the border if he had a problem with proud white people, but I couldn't, and he knew I couldn't, which

Chapter 41   *Church Friend*

emboldened him all the more: A fight at a church function was unthinkable.

Chapter 42

Instigator

Why wasn't I invited? moaned Sean, feigning injured feelings while sitting—somehow suavely—atop his Skyway, one foot casually planted on the ground.

Don't! I didn't know you would want to come, apologetically whined Tracy, the busty, red-bikini-clad hostess of the pool party.

Sean, Corey, Jimmy (kids from my football team) and I had been riding our bikes through the creek all morning. Like the revelers behind Tracy's house, we were soaked: They were wet and oiled while we were covered in mud.

The party was coming to an end when we rode up. Kids scuttled from the back gate in flip-flops, carrying wet towels and bags stuffed with oozing bottles of sun block and glossy magazines, some heading homeward down the street, others impatiently waiting by the curb for their rides.

Is that Jacob? I casually asked the group.

Who are you talking about? answered Corey, twisting around on his bike, flecks and clumps of mud all the way up in his dirty-blond hair.

That kid, there? Two houses down. The one who told the 8th graders about the things I said last year—is that him? I asked as a car honked us out of its way.

Chapter 42　　　　　　　　　Instigator

Yeah that's him, said Jimmy, briefly breaking off his passionate attempt to convince a girl named Shannon to allow him to chauffeur her home on his handlebars.

I had discovered that Jacob was one of the kids who had all but delivered me to the jaws of nonwhite 8th graders the previous year. His unexpected appearance suddenly racked me with indecision. I hadn't considered retaliating against people like Jacob, but the longer I thought about what he had done and the role he had played, the angrier I became.

He and his like are as much to blame as the ones who came after me—maybe more, I reasoned to myself.

But the tone of my inner-voice abruptly shifted.

It's too much trouble to ride after him; he's halfway down the street. He's not worth it.

But he's antiwhite and he'll do it again if I let him get away with it, my thought countered.

He is antiwhite, I agreed.

Taking off on my bike, I turned to my lovesick friends and, not wanting an audience, shot, *I'll be right back.*

A minute later, I caught up with Jacob in his wet bathing suit, untied sneakers, and limp towel hanging over his boney shoulders.

I called his name in a neutral voice. He turned around and immediately lost all the color he had gained earlier in the day.

Jason...Umm...what do you...what's up? he said in a quivering, culpable voice.

Crucible

You're looking pretty guilty, Jacob, I said accusingly, getting off my bike and dropping it in the grass.

No, I... just tired...been in the sun....

In truth, now that I was standing near him, he looked too small and pathetic to fight: no muscles to speak of, nothing up front for his trunks to cling to.

I know you ratted on me last year.

No...I didn't...what are you talkin' about?

Don't lie to me, I casually continued. *I know you ratted me out to the 8th graders.*

No way, he guiltily protested, as a jogger breezed by with his brindled boxer panting by his side, the dog's nails clicking on the sidewalk. *I don't even remember what the conversation was about...it just—came out.*

So you don't know what I'm talking about, but IT just came out?

He half-nodded, half-shook his head, swallowing hard.

Listen, I'm not begging anyone to be fair any more. If kids want to fight me because of what I believe—I'll fight 'em. (I hardened my tone) *So, if you've got a problem with my pride—if you don't like what I have to say and you think you're gonna sic some nonwhite kids on me, then you better be ready for the same ass-kicking they'll get when they come looking for me—you got it?!*

Yeah, yes...I—

I silenced him with an openhanded slap across his face.

Chapter 42   *Instigator*

    He was lying about accidently ratting on me. He had sicced nonwhites on his self-perceived betters more than once. But he was too small and pathetic to punch—just yet: I would've felt guilty for weeks.

    As I rode back to my friends, past the kids who gawked after me, past the speechless adults, and thinking about the fight at noon on the coming Sunday, I fingered the pocket that held my Confederate flag: I was sending a message, I was standing up and saying, "NO MORE!"

Chapter 43

Must be Crazy

'I'll beat the shit out of that bitch,' I was told Reggie blustered while shadowboxing and pacing the room.

By the end of his tirade, Reggie had agreed to fight me at one o'clock on the coming Sunday, fiercely adding that I would leave the tennis courts in a body bag.

You know he's not gonna come alone, warned Rob from behind a slice of pepperoni pizza. Rob was a robustly-built kid whom I had asked to come with me to the courts.

I know he's not, but I'm not worried about that. We'll get there an hour early and wait by the baseball field beside the courts to see how many kids he brings. If he has a friend or two, I'll fight him. But if he brings a gang—or if he brings weapons, we'll leave without them ever knowing we were there.

A few minutes before noon the following day, Rob and I quietly rolled up to the baseball field on our bikes. Though it was a beautiful day, the field and the courts were deserted. I should've felt great, but I couldn't have felt sicker; waiting for a fight was far worse than being in one: My legs were weak, and fear writhed like oiled snakes in my gut.

To get my mind off the fight, Rob and I took turns riding around the baseball diamond as fast as we could. It wasn't until we

Chapter 43 — *Must be Crazy*

reflected on the day's events that we realized how much attention we drew to ourselves.

Are you ready for football? gasped Rob, as a cloud of dirt leapt from his skidding rear wheel and swirled about him, spraying little rocks that skipped nosily along the ground.

Hell, yeah. We start in a couple of weeks.

Actually, getting back on the gridiron was as depressing as it was exciting. Football season meant the start of school and everything awful that school had come to represent. As Rob and I talked, and as my mind catalogued the abuse I would have to endure over the coming school year, we spotted a group of boys riding up to the tennis courts—it was one o'clock.

Keeping a thin stand of oaks, pines and their saplings between us and the newcomers, Rob observed, *There aren't any black kids.*

The group of six or seven, all around my age, rode to the middle of the courts and chatted as they checked their watches and impatiently scanned their surroundings.

Do you know any of 'em? asked Rob, craning his neck, surveying the group.

I don't think so.

Maybe they know where Reggie is?

Maybe, I responded vaguely, worriedly pondering what they were up to.

Let's ride over.

No! I nervously blurted, grabbing his handlebars. *We'll ride around to make sure Reggie isn't hiding with a bunch of friends. Then we'll go over.*

After a quick pass around the forested area bordering the courts, Rob and I cautiously approached the group.

Are you Jason? hollered a lanky boy as we rode up, his voice cracking countertenor mid-sentence.

Who's asking? I hollered back, scanning their hands, waistbands, and pockets for weapons.

We just came to see a fight. We heard some kid named Jason was gonna fight Reggie.

Have you seen Reggie today? I continued as Rob and I rode to a stop, keeping the tennis net between their group and us.

Yeah, answered lanky, *me and Pat* (he shot a glance at a squat boy) *saw him and Lavon an hour ago.*

Did they say anything? I asked, the court's acrid stench of hot rubber forcibly reminding me of a car peeling out.

Reggie said they were waiting for some more of their friends to show up before they rode over here. We figured they'd be here.

I looked at my watch; it was almost 1:30, and there was no sign of Reggie, Lavon, or any of their friends.

The squat boy suddenly piped into the brief silence. *So, you're Jason?*

Yeah, and it looks like Reggie isn't gonna show.

Seems he's too much of a puss to fight you, Rob crowed, his laughter sparking chuckles from the group.

Chapter 43 — *Must be Crazy*

You guys—bleated a freckled-faced boy in a worried sort of voice—*you guys should watch out. Lavon has a switchblade...he said he was gonna stick you with it,* he added, nodding in my direction.

Seriously? I answered, feeling a sudden rush of chills that threw the heat from my skin.

Ideas to placate Lavon soared into my mind unexpectedly, but I swallowed hard and smothered them with my will, mastering my fear.

Are you guys gonna see Reggie and Lavon anytime soon? I asked.

Yeah—lanky and squat chimed—*well, Reggie, at least,* added lanky.

Tell 'em that I'm not gonna give them another chance to gang up on me. And there's no way I'm gonna wait around here for some thug to jump me from behind with a knife.

If Reggie or Lavon still want to fight after pussing out today—tell 'em to let me know, and I'll surprise them on MY time—no knives—just the ass-stomping of their lives.

Everyone knew I stood up for my people, and everyone knew I hadn't lost a fight, but as the sands of summer's freedom ran low, my reputation as a warrior for the Spirit of the West was on the rise.

Neither Reggie nor Lavon accepted my offer, but I did hear back that they were convinced I was insane, and that they had said: '*Crazy crackers ain't worth it.*'

Chapter 44

Pearls Before Swine

My free-time had shrunk as I spent the bulk of my days practicing football with my teammates and father. Once the official team practices started, I wouldn't have any time to myself until the season was over.

With my final night of freedom, I bicycled to a friend's house several neighborhoods away. Bored and gloomy over the end of summer, my friend Stuart and I rode around his neighborhood, lazily looking for something to do.

The day's dying fires caught briefly in the sky, casting pinks and violets that ebbed like receding mists as I followed him toward an unkempt house, its front door agape, a stereo blaring inside, and a slovenly gaggle of kids hanging out in the front yard.

I was talking about football when Stuart cut in, *I know these kids,* as he waved halfheartedly to the group.

What's up, Stuart? chortled a muscular boy whose patchy whiskers made him look older than he was.

What's up Jake? What are you drinking?

Jake was resting a quarter-filled, pale-green plastic cup on his burgeoning potbelly.

Nothin', dip-shit—it's my dip-cup, blurted Jake, launching a long, brown rope of spit that plopped grossly in the cup's dark liquid. *But we got da good stuff right-chere.*

Chapter 44 — *Pearls Before Swine*

Jake edged over to a trashcan and raised a bottle of brown liquor into view.

Taking a hardy swig, he belched, *you two want any?*

No. Thank you, I responded with a tone of thinly-veiled disgust, to which he chuckled moronically.

In addition to Jake, there were about fifteen to twenty kids pointlessly wandering the front and back yards of the house in different states of drunkenness and merriment. There was—to my surprise—no sign that parents, or any adults, for that matter, were present.

A heavy darkness drew around us as we lingered out front, unwilling to go near the house. Bats careened overhead, climbing and diving, snatching their breakfast from the dark sky. A steady stream of kids shuffled and slouched from the backyard to the front, and then back again, and along with Jake, we chatted with some as they meandered.

These were some of the most disheveled kids I had ever met. With the exception of a black boy, whose voice and laughter occasionally howled from the backyard, they were all white, some dotted with bruises, others clad in dirty clothes, all wearing the same empty, nihilist expression.

There aren't any streetlights…and not many stars tonight, I mentioned to Stuart as I studied the sky.

Makes it easier for us to party, snickered a boy with wild, long brown hair, who pointed a finger at me, winked and clicked twice with his mouth.

Crucible

Just then, two portly girls came heavily loping and giggling out of the darkness on the side of the house, their thick legs jiggling and twisting from under their shorts.

What's so funny? shot a pimple-covered boy as though he were angry, dropping his scowl the next moment and laughing, perfectly amused with himself.

Fuck you, Dustin, snapped the blonde irritably.

Oh my gawd, oh my gawd!—started the brunette effusively—*Chrystal's giving Darryl head on the trampoline!*

Everyone laughed except for me—I had no idea what "head" was.

When a few kids noticed I wasn't laughing, Stuart spoke to their puzzled expressions.

Jason probably doesn't like race mixing. I mean, no—he spoke faster in response to their shocked expressions—*it's not like he's racist, but he probably doesn't like race mixing.*

What are you talking about? I confusedly blurted to Stuart as the laughter went silent and some of the boys sidled away, casting fearful glances at the two fat girls as well as a gaunt girl who marched over like the ghost of white genocide.

Seriously?! shot the blonde walrus, leaving her mouth agape as though she were about to eat, or vomit, or eat her vomit.

You've got to be joking, blared the brunette elephant seal, staring searchingly at Stuart and me while barking little bursts of incredulous laughter.

Chapter 44 — *Pearls Before Swine*

I was still confused, but I was not about to back down from a bunch of self-righteous, affectedly aggrieved, antiwhite misfits—so I stared at them, pokerfaced.

The ghost of white genocide, Gaunt, stepped within a few feet and halted. She glared at me with an expression that said—quite clearly—that she would have liked to cut my throat. Her lips were pressed so tightly together they vanished from her anemic face, and the dark wells behind the thin slits of her eyes burned with venomous hatred.

I instantly recognized her fanatical hostility: She was a vicious antiwhite pig, an enemy of the West. Her breathing came in long, deep gasps, which almost whistled through her pencil-thin nose. Everyone regarded her with an anxious gaze as she appeared to struggle with her next move.

Are you serious? You better not be serious, she threatened.

I glared at her as a priest staring down a banshee from Hell.

You...you just try to stop them from being together, she hissed.

I'm not trying to control what anyone does—that's what you antiwhites do. Remember? You tell everyone else how they're supposed to live and what they're supposed to think.

She was outraged. Her little fists clenched tightly by her side as she uttered a soft growl through pursed lips.

So much for tolerance, right? I continued with a scornful tongue, mocking the tantrum she was threatening to throw, a behavior she probably learned from watching her misandrous mother dominate her gelded father. *You so-called egalitarians are hypocrites...the worst authoritarians the world has ever known.*

Racist! she spat like venom from a forked tongue, pathetically stomping one foot before turning and marching back into the house.

No, guys...listen, Stuart interjected placatingly, *Jason isn't a racist—*

It doesn't matter what they think, Stuart. I'm not a follower of their sick faith...I don't submit to crazed feminists—so that makes me a racist, and an anti-Semite, and a hater, and all the other names they call people who disagree with them.

Why do you hate blacks? shot the blonde walrus, her arms ridged by her flanks.

Why do you hate whites? I shot back, unfazed by the antiwhite tactics of arguing.

I'm white—I can't hate whites! she ignorantly retorted, sniggering stupidly to her friends as though she had made a point.

Oh yeah, right—whites can't hate whites, just like Americans can't hate America, or like ditch diggers can't hate digging ditches, or like fat girls can't hate being fat.

Fuck you! she bloodcurdlingly screamed.

No thanks, I quipped, *the doctor said I had to cut back on harmful fats.*

You're gonna...fucking...you're gonna fucking get it, motherfucker, stuttered the brunette elephant seal, pointing a thick finger at me.

Chapter 44 — Pearls Before Swine

I'm not afraid of you scumbags. As a matter of fact...here, take a look at this.

I pulled my Confederate flag from my pocket and the fat girls' faces widened with disbelief, gawking as though I held aloft a severed head. *Now—go away.*

They stampeded off into the house, following the same path taken by Gaunt.

As they disappeared, a third corpulent female, crowned with big brown curls, waddled around from the backyard, wiping her mouth off with her chubby hand. A couple of boys hustled over and roped her into hasty conversation, slipping apprehensive glances in my direction.

I was telling Stuart that I was going to head home when I heard a shout from the front door.

Wasss up, my man? said a large, muscular black boy jovially, smiling broadly. *I'm Darryl. Don't worry bout dhose stupid bitches. Bitches don't know shit,* he added as he crossed the lawn, casting a glance at the curly-haired girl.

Wass up wass up...you want some my gin and juice? he asked me as he nonchalantly approached, brandishing a sports bottle capped by a long, dirty straw.

I declined.

Fuck it. It's empty, he continued, heedlessly throwing it back toward the house.

Dhey came all up into my shit, talkin' bout how you got a rebel flag an' shit—I don't care 'bout dat shit. Eryone's all uptight. Dats your thing, cat. We all got our things...look at Jake, right, he got on panties—he laughed heartily at Jake—*naugh, Jake, I just messen.*

Darryl chuckled with a broad smile, his teeth and eyes contrasting starkly with the dark of the night and the black of his skin.

The guys, including Stuart, roared with laughter at Darryl's jokes and easygoing nature. I even found myself starting to relax as Darryl talked about college and professional football.

So, we straight, Darryl finally said, holding out his hand for a shake.

Yeah, we're cool, I responded, taking his hand in mine.

Chapter 44   *Pearls Before Swine*

The grass felt sharp on my cheek, and its aroma made me think of freshly cut lawns, which spurred confused thoughts about whether or not I had forgotten to mow my parents' backyard. I didn't know why everyone was shouting and laughing, but the pain on the right side of my face meant only one thing.

It felt like I had been asleep for hours, roused much too early, on too little rest, but Stuart later told me that I got up as soon as I hit the ground. Darryl, a southpaw, had tricked me into shaking his hand so that he could get close enough to steal me in the face.

Ouuuuuuuu yeah, you like dat, motha-fucka? You like dat? I'm gonna get dat flag an wipe my ass on it, Darryl shouted in a voice as bestially cruel as his previous had been lightheartedly innocent.

He was pacing side to side like a boxer, thumbing his nose like Cassius Clay, apparently waiting for the crowd to gather before striking again.

A high-pitched whistle echoed painfully in my ears, and my face throbbed where he caught me with the powerful blow. As I looked about, trying to get a grasp on my situation, trying to make Darryl out from the darkness of the night, pain cried from the tendons in my neck—they'd been strained when my head was violently jolted by the punch.

Still dazed, I raised my fists as Darryl exploded through me, tackling me to the ground.

Moving like lightning, he struggled to pin me where I fell.

Crucible

I pulled my right knee up between us. He landed another blow to my face. I heaved him over to my left and we scrambled wildly for control.

In a flash, he was on his feet, throwing a kick to my side as I rose.

I was up, all my thoughts on the pain erupting from my ribs.

Run! a voice screamed in my head. *Beg him to stop—say that you're sorry.*

He was going to win. He was going to take my flag. It didn't matter that he had tricked me. It didn't matter that I'd seek revenge. All that mattered was that these antiwhite pigs would celebrate my defeat and defile my flag.

His fists were up—he dove in, head bobbing, body weaving. I retreated, circling to my right—advancing two steps as he backpedaled four.

I can't let it happen! I can't let them win! I shouted in my head as I fought with my fears, clutching my flag through the pants-leg of my jeans.

And that's when I felt it—the flag aflame in my pocket, igniting a fire within me, the Spirit of the West Himself steeling me for battle.

Darryl lunged forward, swinging for my face: His reach was longer than mine. His fist grazed my chin—another blow glanced off my right eye. I shoved him back and circled to my left—already gulping air, but finally ready to take the fight to him.

Chapter 44 — *Pearls Before Swine*

I stepped forward and jabbed with my left, jabbing again and again as he blocked and swatted my fist away: I held my right in reserve by my cheek, ready to throw for his face the moment it was open.

We broke apart, circled to our right, and came together again. Faking with my right, I threw a left that landed hard on his mouth, forcing his head backward as he grunted painfully from the blow.

His side was open: I twisted my hips, pivoting on the balls of my feet, blasting him with a powerful right hook to the ribs. The punch landed with a thud that folded him around my fist, making him howl in agony.

I followed with a left to his face that he ducked and countered, hitting me hard in the mouth with a cross.

I tasted blood. It coated my tongue and washed over my chin—my bottom lip was torn open.

Exhausted and in pain, my arms shaking and my legs heavy, I knew I couldn't go much longer.

I paused for breath. He launched himself forward, throwing a wild left hook—I stepped back and countered with a right: His black fist flew within inches of my face, but my right landed hard.

Blood streamed from both his nostrils—he pawed at the gore in disbelief: his nose twisted and shattered.

I drove forward—no mercy for the merciless, no pity for the pitiless. A bone-crunching left to his face, a right to his ribs—a left to his exposed belly—he bent forward—I threw an uppercut: all my strength, all my rage, my fist smashing him in the face.

Crucible

His unfocused eyes stared emptily at the sky for the briefest of moments, and then he fell at my feet.

I was gasping for air in the night's humid silence. Nobody spoke. Everybody peered numbly at their neighbors and the limp hulk on the ground.

Startling me, the curly-haired, fat girl threw herself at Darryl's side.

Are you okay?! she fearfully cried, rolling him onto his back and wiping the blood and sweat from his black face with her thick, white fingers.

Backing to the sidewalk, my pain grew as I slowly recovered my breath.

Get the fuck out of here! screeched Gaunt from somewhere in the midst of the crowd. *We don't want you here! Get the fuck out!*

Wearing the wild look of a harridan, she charged from the grayish, nondescript line of onlookers, an arm extended, pointing to the street.

Get the fuck out, she screamed, as though fueled by rabies.

Come any closer, and you're next—pig, I darkly replied.

Stuart rode with me through the empty streets for a while, but neither of us had much to say.

That was the last time I put my flag in peril, the last time that I would let an enemy come so close to stealing it. Thinking the antiwhites had at least a shred of honor, that they could live and let live on any level, had been foolish. I would never be foolish again.

Chapter 45

Blood of Deeds

Salvation was in the word, and the word was written in the blood of deeds. My resistance to the Regime and victories in combat had made me a foolhardy legend among many of my peers. They viewed me with disbelief, as though I were a character who had stepped from the pages of an impossible tale of resistance to antiwhite tyranny.

I had set myself apart with impudence and daring, an agile tongue and ready fists, but when, as an 8th grader, I set foot in that ivory tower of antiwhite vitriol, in that school that functioned as a den of indoctrination, as a shrine to the Idol of antiwhitism in the form of MLK, I was clothed in the flag of my rebellion.

There, emblazoned on the back of an old jean jacket, I declared to the world my resistance to the Regime that would destroy my people: my flag—sewn from shoulder to shoulder, angry like a crimson flame in the darkness of our age, bright like the dawn the night cannot resist.

I had decided I would never foolishly imperil my flag again, but rather than conceal my opposition to antiwhite oppression, I vowed heightened diligence and preemptive defense. Digging through a closet at home, I had found an old jean jacket to serve as my canvas: my Confederate flag across my back, a Stars and Stripes patch for my

Crucible

left breast, and my father's divisional patch from the military for my right shoulder.

The eyes of my world lit upon me in surprise, in disbelief, and in hatred as I marched through the halls as an impossible anomaly to the day's antiwhite tyranny. Expectantly watching me, my peers held their breath: How would people respond? Would the administration move to suspend or even expel me from school? Would the teaching staff scold or even humiliate me in the presences of onlookers. Would the antiwhite nonwhites beat me down, jumping me, ganging up on me, breaking and bloodying my body and face?

Though I couldn't shake the self-doubt, I projected relaxed confidence as I wended through the cramped halls, and that's when Adam and Chris—seeing my jacket for the first time—caught up with me.

Jason! Where'd you get that jacket? said Adam as he pulled alongside me, a note of troubled awe in his voice.

I brushed imaginary dust from my chest and sleeves. *You like it?* I asked hopefully with a short nod, eager to have someone's approval.

Yeah, it's kick-ass, but—he ran his hand through his dark hair—*you're gonna get kicked outta school for wearing it,* he warned heavily, looking to Chris for support.

God...that's the coolest jacket I've ever seen, chimed Chris, gawking with a mixture of surprise and reverence. *But the blacks are gonna bum-rush you,* he added concernedly, with a pained face, sidestepping two boisterous boys walking in the opposite direction.

I understood where they were coming from: They secretly supported me, and as friends, didn't want to see me get hurt. But I couldn't take advice that stemmed from fear or surrender.

I answered in a sterner voice than I intended. *I'm not backing down anymore, dammit. If they don't like it—it's too damn bad.*

Loose comments—the likes of which had followed me all morning—caught up with us from behind:

...Did you see that jacket...

...Holy shit, that's nuts...

...That kid's got a death wish...

...Oh, I know. He's a racist...

Adam shot fretful glances over his shoulder before continuing. *I know, but that's like putting a bull's-eye on your back...the Confederate flag is cool and all, and I know what you're saying, but you're just asking for it by wearing one,* he offered sympathetically.

I frustratingly stopped in mid-stride and turned to face them both. *I don't give a shit. I don't care what they do. If they come after me, I'll fight 'em on every level,* I stormed reflexively, breaking away and heading toward my next class, leaving them dispiritedly behind.

My words were braver than I felt, but I had resolved to be brave—and that's how I was going to act.

Chapter 46

Behind the Mask

Halfway through day one as an 8th grader, I found myself beneath the billboard, the shrine, the larger-than-life picture of the antiwhites' Idol. Still the only image in the Commons, the Idol gazed upon the faithful as a tangible and benevolent deity—calling them to duty in the service of "equality" by way of inequality: quotas, exemptions, set-asides, subsidies. And he glared upon the faithless as a jealous god—his activists shaming, ostracizing, threatening, and bludgeoning dissenters into conversion.

More to the point, the Idol seemed to consider us as a hawk considers its prey from the clouds. And much like the fearsome talons and razor-sharp beak wielded by the airborne predator, the Idol bristled with an assortment of weapons with which to compel conversion and subservience.

But glued to the floor before the face of antiwhitism, I realized that it was nothing more than a mask for something far more sinister. Just as "liberal" and "progressive" were aliases, concealing the antiwhite entity behind the pleasant names, the Idol was one of many masks worn by this monster.

Jewish folklore speaks to the existence of a demon that enters a living body and slowly assumes dominance, possessing all of its faculties, destroying its will, and finally—transforming it into an image of itself. This antiwhite demon, this *dybbuk*, is the nameless

Chapter 46 *Behind the Mask*

beast behind the pleasant names, the faceless demon behind the Idol's face.

What's more, I thought darkly to myself, it's the force behind the monster that Adam had hauntingly alluded to the previous year.

Mr. Köhne, what in the world?! Cribbs had hustled over from somewhere behind me while I bemusedly studied the Idol. *What in the world do you think you're doing wearing that flag?!*

All the faces in this crowded corner of the Commons wheeled—in unison—in my direction.

165

Cribbs stuttered and twitched before thundering in a scornful voice that startled the spectators, *take that jacket off—and give it to me!*

No, sir, I calmly and respectfully replied.

What? What do you mean, no? You can't wear that thing in school. It's offensive.

Mr. Albright and several more kids silently joined the anxious crowd.

The black kids are decked out in their colors—their red, black, and green, and all those Malcolm X shirts that say, 'It's a Black thang. You wouldn't understand.' Those things offend me. If I can't show my pride, then they can't show theirs.

That's ridiculous! Give me that jacket—Cribbs' eyes darted appraisingly at our spellbound audience—*you can have it back at the end of the day, and I—never—want to see it again,* he commanded, his hand out, trembling.

No, sir.

He stepped closer, taking a slow, measured breath. *Jason, I can suspend you for disobeying me.*

I'm never gonna stop wearing this jacket.

His face went taut, his nostrils flared, and fierce determination seethed into flame like coals in his dark eyes. Snarling just above a whisper, he threatened, *Then I'll have you expelled.*

Do what you gotta do, I coldly replied, confident he wasn't an unbiased, impartial person who simply wanted to do the right thing, but a not-so-secret victimizer of my people, an enemy that disguised

Chapter 46 — *Behind the Mask*

his antiwhite hatred and advanced his antiwhite agenda with every noble-sounding excuse imaginable.

Mark my words, Mr. Köhne; you'll leave that jacket at home from now on, or you won't attend this school, he fumed, turning on his heel and marching off through the crowd of kids, who scrambled noisily to get out of his way.

A little later that day, as I waded through a sea of kids in a hall off the Commons, Wolf's scandalized voice reached me as a distant holler, which caused most to turn in his direction.

Jason! Hey! Jason!

When our eyes met, he threw his hands up and his head back, and then he sharply turned, swatting in my direction while flinging me a look of exceeding disgust. Like reeds turning with the wind, my peers turned in my direction: Humiliating me, he taught them an antiwhite lesson in the process.

Both he and Cribbs had defeated me the previous year: They had guilted me, intimidated me, terrorized me into surrendering, and now they both knew I had defied them.

What would they do? How would they respond, now that they knew I had hardened my resolve? Would they call my parents? Would they suspend me before the end of the first day of school, ominously appearing in the doorway of one of my classes, angrily demanding that I go with them—as a criminal, a thought criminal and prisoner?

My fears were not allayed when my day ended without a suspension; rather, I was certain they were planning how they would censor me while making me look like the censor, persecute me while making me look like the persecutor, terrorize me while making me look like the terrorist.

Chapter 47

Pretexts

While some continue to esteem the—old—Virginia, moralized Ms. Joan Brown a few days later in class, ever so quickly and contemptuously raking me with her cold eyes, *states like Virginia and Texas continue to resist social progress in many ways.*

A month earlier, when I saw her name on my class schedule, I recalled that Ms. Joan Brown was the teacher in the library the previous year who had taken a fiercely antiwhite position in an argument with Mrs. Swan.

White, and as antiwhite as a person can be, Ms. Brown was a bitter, self-important, plastic-faced woman who thought herself a genius: Opinionated and ill-humored on the outside, she was as cold and dead as feminism can leave a woman on the inside.

She made no effort to conceal her antiwhite sentiments, which clearly stemmed from her deep-rooted, misandrous psychosis.

What do you mean by social progress—liberal ideology? I said in a mocking tone, causing the eyes of many to go wide with fear of Brown's response. *You know, differences of opinion aren't a bad thing—that's called freedom.*

It's not freedom, Jason; those people are bigots! she scornfully barked, tilting forward as though she were launching her words like spit.

Crucible

It was as if the dybbuk had come ravingly to life within her upon hearing the words of an exorcist—a behavior that I had discovered was nearly guaranteed when using logic and facts in an argument with an antiwhite.

You can't call someone a bigot in this context without being a bigot. The moment you say another person's views are intolerable because those people are intolerant, you become a bigot.

Her face went stupid, confusion and then anger spilled in through the muscles around her eyes and brow as she realized I was right.

Call them whatever you want. She dismissively shook her head and backhanded the air.

Let's be clear, I doggedly continued, *you're talking about white people in Virginia and Texas, right?*

Yes! They discriminate against minorities and women, and they deny women their freedom of choice, she added snappishly, to which a few girls straightened haughtily in their chairs, as though reciting antiwhite superstitions was a checkmate.

Oh, okay, okay—so once everybody is forced to espouse liberal ideology, once no one is permitted to disagree with liberal, progressive opinions, then we have freedom of choice?

Out! barked that antiwhite crusader, Ms. Brown.

She marched heavily to the door, opened it, and stepped into the hall, which caused the room to swell in morbid anticipation of the fate that awaited me.

Chapter 47 *Pretexts*

You will not disrupt my class—do you understand me? she furiously hissed after closing the door behind me. *I've spoken with other teachers about you, and we are not going to tolerate your insolence this year.*

Is that so? I drawled with an indifferent grin, assuming the cockiest pose and demeanor I could summon, knowing it would drive every misandrous bone in her body insane.

Yes—that's right! she spat exasperatedly, newly-formed splotches on her neck and cheeks pulsing feverishly. *This jacket of yours is disgraceful...I....*

She faltered, wanting to say more, but reining in her fury, probably realizing that she was dangerously close to revealing her antiwhite hatred as other than a crusade for noble pretexts.

Taking a deep breath and regaining her composure with the flash of an idea that gleamed wickedly in her eyes, she smiled nastily. In a smug tone, she dismissed me, saying, *I won't be surprised if you get put in your place by one of the upstanding young black men at this school.*

Her tongue regained its edge as she finished, *Now go to the office for the rest of the period.*

Chapter 48

Monster

With a raucous river of bodies hemming me on all sides, I gratefully exited the school's front doors as the day's final bell tolled our release. In the school's lot, a brown Honda Civic idled restlessly on bald tires. Its occupants, four surly-faced teenaged blacks, intently scanned the students sluicing through the building's entrance.

Jason, wait up! shouted Adam's voice from somewhere behind me.

Just yards from the front of the building, I turned and waited for him to emerge from the scuttling mob.

A moment later, he and Chris came bustling into view.

Did you know Cordell was talking about fighting you? asked Adam in an urgent voice.

No. I hadn't heard, I vaguely responded as I shot a glance over my shoulder at the sedan.

A large black boy, Cordell's ire was more than enough to concern me, but something wasn't right about the idling Honda. It looked threateningly out of place. The occupants didn't appear interested in giving anyone a ride home. They were just—scanning.

– Jason—JASON! Did you hear me?

No. Sorry...er. What now? I asked amid the clamorous chatter of students funneling around us like raging waters.

Cordell was—

Chapter 48 — Monster

Stop that right now, Mrs. Peyton squawked from behind Adam at two kids playing tug-of-war with a backpack.

Adam threw a vexed look at Peyton before continuing. *Cordell's trying to get blacks and Mexicans to help him jump you.*

He weighs three of me. Why does he need help?

Who knows—what are you looking at?

What...nothing, I lied, knitting my brow and unconcernedly shaking my head.

The sedan was crawling through the lot like a big cat stalking its prey; the occupants, still scanning the thinning crowd, hadn't picked anyone up for a ride home.

I didn't know it then, but I was told the following day that Lamont Riddick had been one of the four blacks in the car. At nearly 18-years-old, he was a sophomore at the high school down the street. About three inches taller and a lot burlier than me, Riddick (he went by his last name) had an infamous reputation for violence, criminality, and for ruthlessly carrying out his threats. He was also known for his personal mission, which he declared was to avenge his people, to make the "colonialists" suffer, to make white America suffer, to *gat* all the "racists" for what they had done to his people.

At one of his suspension hearings, his mother, a black-Hispanic woman, was heard shouting that the high school administration was racist, that America was a racist country that needed to pay for its past.

America—white America—paid for the government housing she and Riddick lived in. We paid for the healthcare they received. We paid for their meals, their financial welfare, Riddick's education, and the infrastructure, policing, and emergency services they used and relied on. What more would she have us do? If not cash, civility, medicine, housing, food, and education, in what currency was she demanding we pay our "debt?" In blood?

When Riddick heard about me and my Confederate jacket, he vowed he would get me, that he would hunt me down no matter how long it took, and that when I had no place left to hide, he was going to *blind the racist* and *burn his jacket.*

A realization gripped me like an iron maiden: This was the monster Adam had fearfully predicted would come for me—the dybbuk's beast. The one to whom my opinions warranted unspeakable violence. The one who would pursue me to the end.

Chapter 49

F in White Privilege

Mrs. Sargent posted herself at the front of the class, her gestures and the look on her face electrically alive with an unnatural giddiness.

Class, today we have the distinct honor of hearing from Dr. Heidi McIntyre.

Mrs. Sargent fawningly tilted toward McIntyre, beaming at her with a look of deep reverence, prompting my peers to self-consciously shift themselves into the most respectful poses they could muster.

Clad in a blue pantsuit, McIntyre was a beefy woman with an androgynous face, and she appeared to be hungrily eyeing my female classmates.

Dr. McIntyre is an activist and champion for social and gender equality. She's written influential articles and lectured students and professionals at all levels. She's organized workshops...um—Sargent paused, slipping on her glasses and bringing an index card up to her face, her eyes darting between her notes and the class—*she's consulted with many educational institutions...she's worked with other pioneers in the field to create curricula, teaching methods, and climates that are gender fair and multicultural.*

The programs she's built focus on the inclusive process, and those materials help teachers—like myself—to foster and maintain social and gender equality in the classroom. She's won many awards and she's been recognized for distinguished leadership in education.

Lowering the index card and sliding her glasses from her nose, Sargent reverentially continued. *She's a teacher's teacher. And with her most recent endowment from the Rothstein Fund*—she and McIntyre exchanged knowing smiles—*she is able to be with us today.*

You will give her the utmost respect and attention a person of her achievement and stature deserves, Sargent ordered, her tone and demeanor shifting ever so slightly, subtly but threateningly revealing the real Mrs. Sargent below the pleasant exterior: a tyrant who tolerated no deviation from the Regime's antiwhite orthodoxy.

As the class fawningly applauded and McIntyre began her lecture, I lapsed into the recent news that Cordell was recruiting nonwhites to jump me, and that Lamont Riddick was going to blind me and burn my jacket. But my fears were slowly eclipsed by McIntyre's vile sermon: It was the purest antiwhitism I had ever heard.

McIntyre railed against Western Civilization. She arrogantly sermonized about society's structure, bludgeoning us with the ridiculous notion that it was intentionally designed to benefit whites at the expense of nonwhites.

Like a hermaphroditic high priestess of the new antiwhite religion, she loftily affirmed that the institutions themselves were "racist," and as a consequence, white people (willingly and unwillingly) unfairly benefited from invisible advantages she called *white privilege.*

Most of the class appeared hypnotized by her antiwhite venom, but I was furious—and Mrs. Sargent knew it. She repeatedly threw me the "dreaded" evil-eye as McIntyre self-importantly fumed and belched like a smokestack against everything I held dear. Sargent knew what I was thinking. She knew I wanted to defend my people and Western Civilization. With every fiber of her being she attempted to intimidate me by bristling with female aggression, narrowing her eyes to bulldoze me, as she likely bulldozed her cringing, obedient husband.

But I ignored her "terrifying" display. I wanted to pay close attention to McIntyre's antiwhite propaganda. With a thick, otherworldly glaze sluggishly crawling over her small, sharp eyes, McIntyre avowed—in a religious fervor—that all whites are "racist," that even she was an unwitting "racist," that we might not actively think "racist" thoughts or commit "racist" acts, but we are, nonetheless, inherently "racist." And, consequently, it is our moral duty to dig deep into ourselves and society to uncover our "racism," admitting it, owning it. Only then, she solemnly declared, can we cure this *horrific blight.*

She wasn't finished, but I raised my hand and began speaking.

I have a question.

Jason, hissed Sargent from her desk as if she were perched in a guard tower with a rifle, scowling in the ugliest face she could pull.

Crucible

We may have time for questions when I'm finished, frowned McIntyre as though she wanted to silence me with a ball gag, the scent of her antiwhite man-hatred wafting about the room like ozone from a rusty power transformer, buzzing and snapping dangerously.

I just want to make sure I understand before we move on, I innocently enough proceeded.

Jason! growled Sargent, bringing her hands down hard on her desk with a sharp clap, rising from her chair like a great pear-shaped balloon coming to life.

So, I doggedly continued, turning back to McIntyre, *our white privilege is—invisible?*

That's correct, she hesitantly answered, sensing a trap, casting an apprehensive eye at Sargent.

And if whites achieve financial and professional success—the success is evidence of our invisible white privilege, right?

The thing about white privilege.... She glanced around at the faces in the room, stalling. *When whites are successful...it's not entirely due to white privilege, but....* She was slowly regaining her pompous confidence, inflating like a blowfish. *We can say—yes, we can absolutely say that it plays a determining role.*

Okay, sure, so when whites are successful, it's a product of invisible racism, not talent or genius or hard work—

I think you've said enough, she sharply cut in, deepening her voice to sound as threatening as possible.

I'm not finished.

Chapter 49 F in White Privilege

McIntyre shook her head dictatorially. *You're depriving your classmates—(You are finished, Jason,* seethed Sargent's voice from the direction of her desk)—*of the information I'm here to share with them.*

Glancing at the gargoyle who used to be Mrs. Sargent, I turned back to McIntyre.

One more thing, whites are racist even if we don't do or say anything racist—because the racism that's in us is also invisible, right?

Yes, she coldly responded.

So we're pretty much always guilty no matter what we do?

Yes, but—

According to you, we have a lot to feel guilty about—which means we have a lot to do to make up for our invisible crimes.

Be quiet, Jason, harshly threatened Sargent, but I continued to ignore her.

How can inanimate objects, like institutions, be racist?

It's a sophisticated subject—

Explain it. I'd like to hear the evidence.

It's complicated—

Apparently. You—(Just stop, pleaded a girl's voice from somewhere behind me)—*You say it's our moral duty to tear racism out of ourselves and society, but what if people don't believe we're guilty? Does that make them immoral?*

Crucible

After a long pause, during which McIntyre seemed to be sizing me up and coming to a very ugly, irreversible conclusion, she finally breathed, *Yes.*

Is it racist if whites aren't submissive to nonwhites? I spat, becoming heated.

Maliciously squinting so as to shoot "horrifying" feminine darts at me, she intoned in a singsong voice as though she were an Orthodox Christian priest, *It can be a sign of deeply held racist views.*

Lady –

Jason! shouted Sargent, rattling my classmates.

Lady (I stood up and grabbed my book-bag), *if we lived in a sane country, you'd be in a straightjacket—not abusing us with your bullshit.*

Sargent grabbed my arm as I walked through the door, saying loud enough for all to hear, *You just earned yourself an F on this assignment, and I'm calling your parents.*

As I walked away and the door swung shut behind me, the last thing I heard was McIntyre telling the class, *That was an example of the kind of hatred we need to eradicate.*

Chapter 50

Honing

Several weeks later, Lamont Riddick was still pursuing me: He had approached two kids at a McDonalds in Fairfax, asking them about where I hung out after school; he had asked some girls at a party in Vienna if they knew me, and if I partied there on the weekends; and he had offered several boys $50 if they would lure me to play a game of basketball in Centreville.

I had seen the dirty Honda numerous times as it stalked through the streets after school, its occupants hunting for me like impatient African poachers. I watched as they sped in random directions, slowing down as they approached groups of kids and then taking off, prowling from road to road.

Their searches had been totally random, presumably because they didn't know where to look. But their patrols had recently narrowed, focusing on the routes I took, which meant they had discovered—at the least—the general area in which I lived.

I didn't know what to do about Riddick. He was bigger, stronger, fiercer, and a hardened fighter. He would beat me in a fight. His gang would likely help him. He would blind me and burn my jacket as he had vowed. Plus, I had to worry about Cordell and the crew he was assembling to jump me in school. And now—with the exception of Jacob, who had been reformed by my promise to do to him what I would do to the attackers he inspired—some of the white kids who had deliberately piqued the nonwhites with talk about my "racism" and "hate" the previous year were at it again.

There was so much going on, I didn't know what to do, but I figured I had to take care of the threats within the school before dealing with Riddick. To avoid him in the meantime, I varied the routes I took home as well as the times I left school. Often, I stayed late, wandering the empty grounds until all was clear, periodically catching sight of the Honda zigzagging here and there, fruitlessly

Chapter 50   *Honing*

searching for me. Occasionally, I left before the day was over, sneaking off the school's lot, skipping the final period or two.

When should I skip out today? a thought asked, as I apprehensively stared through a rain-battered window at a pine tree buffeted by winds that beat its branches in angry fits, its crown framed by low, smoky clouds tumbling across the sky under a black roof, white-veined by lightning. *What am I gonna do about Cordell...and what about these self-abasing, white pigs stirring things up again?*

Ms. Brown was lecturing the class on the "Civil War" and, of course, black slavery. I snapped out of my contemplation when her voice cut into my mind like thinning shears.

...we're all responsible for the social wounds caused by slavery.

I raised my hand and began speaking—she never called on me.

So blacks are responsible, too? I asked in thinly camouflaged sarcasm.

A girl sitting to my left shot me a nervous glance.

Obviously not, Brown snorted backhandedly, coughing on a short, mocking laugh.

Yeah, I didn't think so, I muttered, ready to drop the issue when I suddenly had a thought.

Ms. Brown, Paul's parents—I tipped my head in Paul's direction, a white boy from one of the Eastern Bloc countries—*fled from the leftists in the Soviet Union* (Brown simpered at me with the mocking maturity of a nine-year-old), *so since they're new to America, are they responsible, too?*

Of course—Paul and his family weren't here during the Civil War, but we all unfairly benefit from the long-term effects of slavery.

Black slavery ended in 1865! How in the hell do whites benefit today?!

I knew I had crossed another line; I was back-talking another adult. It wasn't me. It wasn't how I had been reared—my parents would be furious.

One more outburst like that and I'll send you to the office again, she heatedly snapped.

Enraged and unable to tolerate another minute of her antiwhitism, I leapt to my feet, my arm outstretched, pointing a damning finger at her ugly face.

You believe the war was fought over slavery, right?! If that's the case, how many white men died to free the blacks?! Well?! How many?! Hundreds of thousands! Hundreds of thousands of white men died for them! And how many more whites died ending slavery around the world?!

We don't owe the nonwhites, I shouted, *they owe us!*

All of Brown's pretentious bravado and affected self-righteousness disappeared in a flash, and for the first time in my life I saw cracks in the monolith of antiwhite power.

How many trillions of the white man's dollars have been spent on welfare programs for nonwhites all over the world?! How many of the white man's inventions have gone to ease the suffering and better

Chapter 50 — Honing

the lives of nonwhites all over the world?! Answer me! I yelled, almost uncontrollably.

I had never felt so disgusted by an adult, so utterly contemptuous, so ready to put an end to her tyranny.

How many jobs and loans and raises and promotions and admissions to universities have been stolen from whites and given to nonwhites who didn't deserve it—simply because of their race?! Well? How many, Ms. Brown?!

That's hate speech! she suddenly screeched like a howler monkey, puffing herself up even as she appeared to be shrinking. *That's the kind of thing that hate-mongers write in dirty little pamphlets—*

It's love speech, and I'm a love-monger, I laughed at her, mocking her antiwhite evasion.

It's hate speech, and I won't allow you—

I don't care what you won't allow, I yelled over her, fury filling me like magma speeding through a volcano. *I'm sick of it! I'm sick of you! You can take your antiwhite trash and shove it up your ass!*

As the class gulped air in shock, I knew I would be forced to do several long detentions for my behavior. I knew the administration would make another effort to stop me from wearing my jacket, but I didn't care: The antiwhites had been waging war against my people and the West for the whole of my life—and I had had enough.

When I left the stunned-silent classroom, the jaw-dropped girls appeared horrified, but some of the boys looked as though they wanted to cheer and give me high-fives as I passed. It was a victory, and as I left the room, my flag on my back blazed with a message which few could have accurately read in its power and beauty: I had only just begun to fight.

Chapter 51

Loyalties

I was considering joining a new church, as mine was increasingly antiwhite. The church elders had even taken me aside to discourage my defense of our people.

Actually, I was very near to turning my back on organized Christianity. All the churches I had attended had been the same. They all had preached and praised passivity as the "moral" way to deal with an enemy. And they all had adopted antiwhitism's version of history and codes of right and wrong.

Some of the members of my church even abetted nonwhites living illegally in the area—*after all,* they melodramatically lectured, as though wrapped in ivory robes and speaking down from the cross, *we're all God's children.* As these hypocritical, self-righteous Christians were also antiwhite, it was immensely unsurprising when they *lacked the resources* to aid the few, struggling white immigrants living legally in the area.

Though Daren's mother and live-in boyfriend, Miguel, rarely made eye contact or spoke to me after I started defending the West at church, their disapproval didn't change my relationship with Daren. He knew who I really was, how I really felt. He knew I wasn't any of the things the antiwhites baselessly and calculatingly claimed about me. He knew I was only defending my people's dignity—which

Crucible

included half his heritage—against the bogus accusations by the antiwhites.

Unfortunately, Daren, Adam, and Chris were the only three who showed me any goodwill and friendship. Unlike the previous year, not even my record-setting season on the football field did anything for my likability. Few people talked to me, and Fox, whom I had seen several times at school, would change direction when she saw me: I was told that she thought my interest in her was *gross*.

Aside from Daren, Adam, and Chris, no one at church or school cared that my birthday had come and gone, marking the 14th year of my life. Nobody else spoke more than a sentence or two to me, not even Mark or Kevin, or Greg or Ian. And things were about to get even worse.

Adam, Chris, Daren and I were eating our lunches at school when Zack, a quiet boy who would occasionally pop and bubble with inappropriate energy at the lunch table, broached *race war*.

SO WHAT IF—what if there's a race war, Jason? asked Zack provokingly, as several kids stopped in mid-chew to listen in. *You know, between whites and minorities…like, what if minorities started killing every white person they saw—and a race war started? And you can't,* he bounced excitedly in his seat, *and you can't say there isn't going to be one—you have to choose a side.*

Why are you asking? shot Chris, an investigative note in his voice.

Chapter 51 *Loyalties*

Chris and I exchanged looks that said Zack's question was suspicious.

Who would you fight for? pressed Zack, almost eagerly, eyes popping out of his unnaturally narrow face.

Are you nuts? I said, giving him a piercing stare. *I can't even imagine a race war* (Zack shook his head stupidly, about to interrupt, about to say that I couldn't deny the prospect of race war), *but if nonwhites started killing every white person they saw, you better believe I'd fight for the West.*

What about you, Daren? schemingly asked Zack with a wry smile, his head pointed at me but his wide eyes aimed at Daren.

He'd fight with me—obviously, I blustered indignantly, stricken with concern for Daren's feelings, with the worry that he was hurt by the implication that he wouldn't fight for the West just because he was half black.

I felt myself becoming furious. Daren and I were close. Asking if he would fight against me was outrageous. Besides, almost all his friends were white, he was half white, and his black father wanted nothing to do with him. There wasn't a chance in hell he'd fight against the West and the white race, especially if nonwhites started the war by killing every white person they saw.

I glared at Zack, but I noticed he was still looking at Daren, and more importantly, I noticed that Daren hadn't responded.

I turned to him, and he averted his eyes, staring fixedly at his mashed potatoes, struggling with a semblance of guilt that pulled at his features.

Well, who would you fight for? Zack's voice asked Daren, his words muffled by a thickening fog in my head.

I stared searchingly at Daren's profile as the sounds of the cafeteria grew faint, waiting for him to speak his answer even as I read it on his face.

You would fight against me? I heard myself ask in an empty voice, betrayal's awful blade piercing my heart.

Daren didn't raise his head; he didn't look at me. *I'd fight for my people*, he mumbled to his lunch tray.

Your people? I repeated dazedly. *You're half white—and what about all your white friends*, I asked anxiously, ice-cold, fear-induced adrenaline rushing through my muscles and painfully twisting my stomach as I worried over our friendship.

How could you help the nonwhites if they started killing whites? What about your mom? She's white. I continued desperately, wishing he were joking, but knowing he wasn't, fearing the words he'd say.

He lifted his head abruptly and looked at me with a face I didn't recognize, a face I'd never seen before.

She'd fight for the minorities, too, he said, almost coldly. *America has kept minorities from doing things and being great. It would be better if everyone was mixed and there were no races or cultures to fight over.*

His voice had finality to it, a knowing that he had crossed a terrible line by revealing his allegiance to those who would wage race war against my people.

Chapter 51 *Loyalties*

I was paralyzed with confusion and hurt. I thought I knew Daren, knew how he'd act in a pinch. And now, staring at him as he hardened his features, I realized how wrong I'd been.

Open mouthed, wanting to say more, wanting to beg him to reconsider, I sank into my thoughts as the feeling of loss spilled painfully through every pore of my body: How could a person who had been so close to me, whom I had trusted, make himself into a weapon to smash all I held dear?

I numbly gathered my things, and I thought I heard Adam and Chris gently encourage me to follow them as the cafeteria emptied.

That day—I left the Church, and Daren and I never spoke again.

Chapter 52

Equal Treatment

...true, but you're eventually gonna have to do something about Riddick—he's not giving up. What then? asked Chris, throwing his feet on the back of a chair in the vacant theater's dim light.

I've no idea, I shrugged.

You think they're still in the parking lot? asked Adam, attempting but failing to disguise the worry in his voice.

No. I doubt it. It's been like, what—fifteen minutes since school let out? They normally take off by now.

I still think you should go to the cops, Adam advised doggedly. *He said he was gonna blind you...that's serious shit.*

Right—they'd probably arrest me for provoking him, I said bitterly, hoisting myself up on the lofty stage across from where Adam and Chris reclined in the second row.

He's right, nodded Chris, turning to Adam, and then, *or even if they didn't yell at him, they wouldn't care that Riddick threatened him—Jason's white.*

What's that, sir? continued Chris, putting on an official voice, *you say Lamont Riddick wants to beat you to death? Well, I guess you better stop provoking him with opinions he doesn't like.*

True, conceded Adam, lifting his brow and raising his focus to the crimson stage curtains.

Chapter 52   *Equal Treatment*

We sat in a moment of thoughtful silence before Adam continued.

What are you gonna do about Cordell, then? He's still trying to get kids to help him jump you.

Why aren't they helping him? I asked, perplexed that he hadn't been able to put together a mob—it would have been easy last year.

Your reputation as a kick-ass fighter, Adam snorted.

Everyone knows about your fights, Chris energetically added, *how you knocked those kids out.*

Yeah, but—I shook my head doubtfully—*I don't know...Cordell's pretty huge.*

You might not have a choice, warned Chris, giving me a tragic look.

What about all the kids who talk trash about you—stirring things up? continued Adam, as Chris dropped his feet and leaned forward.

You mean the white kids? I asked.

Yeah—Seth—Jordy—

And Alexa—Roy—Tobin, added Chris, ticking the names off on his fingers while Adam nodded at him.

Yep—and Mandy from Earth Science, said Adam before turning back to me. *And a few more.*

I stood up, poised on the edge of the stage as I stared into the theater's empty darkness.

It's time for me to do something about them, I muttered, almost to myself, feeling as though my path was as dangerous as the darkness was impenetrable.

I'll deal with the boys first—if the girls aren't silenced by what I do to them, I'll cross that bridge when I come to it.

What are you gonna do? asked Chris, his brow knitted.

I'm gonna make it costly to agitate against me. If they want to see me beat-down because I love our people and the West, they'll have to pay for it.

Are you gonna fight ALL of them? choked Adam, a thick texture of worry in his voice.

Deadly resolve spoke through me as I turned cold eyes on my friend.

If I have to.

Do you FUCKING understand?! I shouted at Tobin through gritted teeth, pinning him to a locker, my left hand wrapped tightly around his throat, my right fist drawn back threateningly.

Purple-faced, Tobin, "the rat" as he was known for his self-serving habit of ratting on classmates, nodded as a large group of stunned-silent kids looked on.

One more fucking word about how I need to get my ass kicked because I'm a racist—one more fucking word about Southerners needing to die, and I'll beat the shit out of you.

I pulled him from the locker by his throat, and grabbing his belt with my free hand, I threw him to the floor.

Chapter 52 — Equal Treatment

My gaze darted to another antiwhite boy who scrambled through the crowd in the direction of the office, and then I turned gloweringly back to Tobin. Stepping closer to him, I read in his face the abject hatred and honorless spite of the degenerate, but I also saw fear, his absolute confidence that I would retaliate if he continued agitating against me.

Regarding each other with disdain, I stood over him as a vengeance he and his fellow travelers had made inevitable.

Tell all the other antiwhite pigs that it's over; tell them I'm coming for them.

Days later: *Okay! Okay!* quickly gasped Jordy, spinning around and standing weak-kneed in the middle of the hall, his hands on my chest as two startled black girls eagerly watched.

Did you really think you could outrun me—chump? I demanded.

He shook his head in short, sharp movements while one black girl urgently whispered to the other.

You're pretty tough when you're telling nonwhites what a hater I am.

No, he energetically popped, slowly retreating as I slowly advanced, *I didn't think—*

Shut the fuck up!

I grabbed him by his shirt collar and shook him like a dead fish.

His mouth moved wordlessly, and the black girls giggled.

Crucible

You're a filthy antiwhite pig—do you know that?!

Silver-dollar eyed and slack-jawed, he nodded.

He nodded! one black girl chortled through her fingers, and they shrieked with hilarity.

Are you gonna talk trash about me—EVER—again?

N…no…no, I promise, he stammered.

Several days later: *Where is he?* I coldly asked Adam and Chris as I rounded a row of lockers just minutes after the day's final bell.

He's right over there with a group of friends, said Chris, peering over the crowd while Adam fidgeted by his side.

Seth, a pompous antiwhite boy known for bullying emaciated 7th graders, was standing in a tight circle with five of his antiwhite friends, surrounded by a shifting sea of students.

Cutting through those waters like a warship at ramming speed, I closed on the unsuspecting group. Voices in the crowd went silent and faces turned in my direction with every step I took.

Out of the way, I growled at the three in the circle who had their backs to me.

They scuttled off to the sides, the circle's two girls eyeing me haughtily until I stared them down, apprehension whipping the haughty looks from their homely faces.

The word had spread that I was avenging myself against the antiwhite pigs who agitated against me, but some of them, like Seth,

Chapter 52 — *Equal Treatment*

didn't care: The antiwhite administration supported them, infusing them with a sense of power—license and inviolability.

So—Seth, I said, glaring at him witheringly.

Seth didn't respond. Wearing a deadpan mask, he was likely weighing the effect of his response on his reputation, especially as the questioning faces of his friends looked on.

Voices hurdled over my shoulders from behind.

Jason's gonna fight Seth!

Let me see....

Watch out....

Don't push....

I stepped closer.

You think you can talk trash about me and get away with it?

His eyes darted to the two girls at his left before he spoke.

I'll say what I want, he blustered, an arrogant, antiwhite sneer yanking one of his cheeks into a dimple.

Is that so? I asked, and he nodded.

Speaking slowly, my words were heavy with muffled rage.

When you talk trash about me, I get jumped. From now on, I'm treating your words like punches. So the next time you attack me— I raised my voice—*I'm gonna stomp the shit out of you! You got it?!*

I'll say what I want, he jeered like a broken record, making a mocking sound with his throat as he grinned stupidly, so I slapped him so hard he came off his feet and hit the floor.

Crucible

Before anyone could react, I grabbed him by his shirt and yanked him upright, pinning him to a locker amid the gasps and cries of, *Oh my god!* and *Holy shit!* and *I wanna see!*

His left cheek was already glowing, spider-webbed scarlet lines rising angrily through his flesh.

Do something! screeched one of the antiwhite girls, Britney, to the three antiwhite boys in their group, waving her hands erratically, causing her kinky, light-brown hair to bounce comically.

My left hand against Seth's chest, I turned to my right and pointed an angry finger at the antiwhite pig.

If you instigate anyone against me, you'll get the same treatment he's getting—I pulled Seth away from the locker and slammed him back into it—*you got it, pig?!*

She looked at me with a face of a thousand horrors: The reality had suddenly hit her that if I didn't restrain my own hand, she had no power to stay it—the reality that her strength went only as far as I allowed it.

But I'm a girl, she protested, nearly speechless.

You're the enemy, I countered coldly.

Fixing the three antiwhite boys with an angry glare, I asked if they wanted to be next; they shook their heads and backed up, melting into the crowd.

So—Seth, let's start over—

His face had become livid. He was breathing deeply, balling his fists.

Chapter 52   *Equal Treatment*

Looks like you want a fight, I snarled, slapping and then backhanding him while keeping him pinned to the locker.

Blood leapt from his nose, and it glisteningly flowed over his lips and chin as the fight sped from his eyes.

Leaning in, I breathed coarsely in a lethal voice, *I'm no scrawny 7th grader—you can't push me around. One more antiwhite word about me and I won't be so nice next time. Understand?*

He nodded, and I released him.

A couple days later: *Jason...Jason,* called Roy, a puny, antiwhite white boy who had regularly disparaged me as a bigot and anti-Semite.

With our gym teacher in full view, he jogged over.

I'm really, really sorry about the things I said about you, he nervously explained. *I mean...I just don't want you to be pissed at me, okay? I'm really, really sorry....*

So you're not gonna talk trash about me anymore? I calmly answered him, wondering if it were some sort of trick, putting the gymnasium wall behind me as I scanned the crowd.

No...No way. To be honest...if you want, I'll tell you who does—if you want me to.

I was shocked. Roy was actually offering to sell out other antiwhites to curry favor with me.

Seeing an opportunity, I asked, *Do you know any others who would be willing to keep an ear out for me—let me know who's talking trash and who might be plotting against me?*

Sure—I can look around, he said briskly.

If you're serious, and you do this for me—I'll forgive you.

He smiled broadly.

And you know what—if anybody messes with you or pushes you around, let me know, I added as we parted.

Within days, I had established a small network of informants, to which I also extended my protection. All agitation against me—by white kids—ceased abruptly.

Chapter 53

Turning Tide

Visibly news-heavy, Chris leaned toward me and whispered, *You know Demont?*

Yeah, I whispered back, keeping a close eye on our math teacher's back as she squeakingly scrawled on the whiteboard, the smell of dry-erase ink nauseatingly floating over me.

Demont was a black transferee. He had been expelled from his previous school for some sort of criminal behavior. As he had savagely beaten a kid since his transfer, some nonwhites had openly hoped he would target me.

I was in home economics this morning, and Keisha asked Demont if he was gonna fight you because of your jacket, continued Chris under his breath, a funny, coy little smile playing at the edges of his lips.

I shot an appraising glance at the teacher and then a curious one at Chris.

And?

He said he wasn't because you guys had talked—

What? I croaked disbelievingly, causing the teacher to spin around, which for her wasn't an easy feat as she was grossly overweight.

Like perfect, grinning angels, Chris and I were vertical in our seats before her grimace swept the room like a menacing searchlight over the grounds of our thought prison, scanning for incriminating faces.

No talking! she thundered at the class in her unusually disturbing voice, and turning back to the whiteboard, found that her wayward arm-meat had sliced an obliterating streak through her examples.

She growled to herself and resumed her numbing lecture.

I've never spoken to him—what's he talking about?

I thought you hadn't. He's just scared to fight you. It's unbelievable, but you're really beginning to turn things around—

CHRIS—JASON! shouted our eardrum-piercing pedagogue. *Do you both want to be sent to the office?*

Startled, we stiffly straightened ourselves and rendered our apologetic attention.

I'll send you both straight to the office this instant, and I'll recommend detention!

When it came to whites misbehaving, she always flew into conniptions. But when nonwhites misbehaved, she daintily asked them to observe her rules.

Like many of the other white antiwhites who prowled like faux-haloed demons through the halls, she styled herself as a moral champion, fervently believing that doing "good" for nonwhites was the greatest good that a person could do. She and her ilk beamed with the joy of self-righteousness when they spoke about the "good" they had done or supported for nonwhites.

Chapter 53 *Turning Tide*

But never did they beam so incandescently as when they inflicted wounds on their own white race while in the process of doing "good" for others. There was no mistaking that they believed harming our people in the process of doing "good" for nonwhites was not only a form of penance, but a fundamental proof of their own righteousness: Who but the righteous would do good for others, and who more righteous than those who would inflict wounds on their own kind for the "good" of others?—so stumbled their idiotic thought process.

As she was not very bright, I used reverse psychology.

Yes, I interrupted her jiggling rant, *I would like to be sent to the office.*

Staring at me like I was a meal that had jumped from her plate and dashed for the door, she indignantly blasted, *Well, I'm not letting you! You just sit right there and keep quiet!*

With a feigned note of defeat in my voice, I shrugged, *Yes, ma'am.*

Chapter 54

Allies Within

I was closing my locker when Mrs. Swan walked over wringing her hands, a resolved expression on her face.

Jason, I know you have only a minute before the bell, but I needed to speak with you, she said in a mother's worried tone.

Her voice was unsteady. She glanced over my shoulders, and she opened her mouth twice to speak, only to close it and start over.

Of course…I haven't spoken to you about your jacket and the statement you're making—the stance you're taking, but I wanted you to know that I disagree with how you're portrayed by some in the administration and teaching staff.

I couldn't believe what I was hearing. No authority figure had acknowledged that I was misrepresented. They had always pompously characterized their antiwhite opinions as universally endorsed, opposed only by the worst of humanity.

I know, she continued clumsily, leaning in and further lowering her voice, *what you really stand for…and I—I want you to know I respect what you're doing. But* (her eyes took on a fearful urgency and she wagged her finger at me) *I don't want you to repeat anything I've just said to you. You couldn't possibly understand what they would do….*

Chapter 54 *Allies Within*

What I mean to say—she paused, searching for words as the bell rang and we found ourselves alone in the Commons—*I just...I support you*, she whispered, so softly I had to read her lips.

I was speechless. She supported me? All this time, as the media and school made me feel utterly alone, alone in my opinions, alone in my concern for the wellbeing of my people, and one in their midst secretly supported me?

I feel—she paused again as the silence in the Commons crowded in around us, *I feel—in many ways, the same way you do about what's happening to...well, to our people, quite frankly—and our heritage. But you mustn't breathe a word of this. I would lose my job—I would lose my health insurance*—her eyes lost their focus—*my car loan...my mortgage....*

She fixed me with a panicked look. *You don't understand—they ruin you if they discover you disagree with them. I wouldn't be able to find comparable employment if they smeared me.*

I won't say anything. I promise, I assured her, utterly dazed and honored by the trust she was placing in me.

I know you won't—and thank you, she smiled relaxingly, patting my elbow.

I'm worried about you, Jason. I know some of your peers pressure you, and I know some of the minority children want to fight you. I hope you're being careful.

I am. Please don't worry—I'll be fine, I said, wanting to alleviate her concern.

Jason, listen to me, she whispered emphatically, her features gripped by sudden earnestness. *Some of the staff have conspired against you all year. They mean business. It's truly dreadful* (she shook her head), *but they've tacitly encouraged students to act violently against you by making inflammatory comments*, she revealed, nodding in response to the disbelief on my face, pursing her lips in disgust, *and they've been discussing how they might expel you. Don't—give—them—a reason. They'll use it to ruin you. One of them even half-seriously suggested that the administration should fabricate a reason to expel you for the good of the student body.*

My mouth fell open. I knew the antiwhites were waging an unrestrained war against my people, that they were doing whatever it takes to win, but hearing about their scheming petrified me.

They've spoken with the superintendent of Fairfax County schools, and I believe they've spoken to the police—

The police, I gasped, wide-eyed with disbelief and fear.

Just don't give them a reason—

I know, but—

Mr. Köhne, lazily drawled a dreaded voice from behind me, sending painful chills through my body as Mrs. Swan flinched, blinking hard in surprise.

Hello Mr. Cribbs, said Mrs. Swan, recovering quicker than me from the shock.

I see you're still wearing that jacket, sneered Cribbs as he strolled over, giving me a disdainful smile.

Chapter 54 — Allies Within

Yeah, I choked, knowing that Cribbs was probably one of the administrators conspiring against me.

You know, you would be well advised to leave it at home. Everyone's getting the impression you're a racist, he continued in a tone of bogus concern.

I've also heard several reports of you intimidating fellow students simply because they disagree with your—how shall I say (he gave a mocking little chuckle)*, your views.*

I stared at him, my heart rate slowly returning to normal.

Humph, he mumbled, smugly twisting his mouth in an *I thought so* expression when I didn't answer him.

So, what's going on here? he asked in a business-cold note, turning to Mrs. Swan.

She didn't look like she knew what to say, like her mind had gone blank.

He would become suspicious of her. The administration would discover her concern for our welfare and culture. She would lose her job and her financial stability.

She was just telling me what a disgrace it is for me to wear my jacket, I said quickly.

Cribbs turned slowly in my direction, throwing his brown suit-jacket open as he placed his hands on his hips.

A hungry smile broke on his face.

I nodded, *she said that I should leave the jacket at home.*

Well, Samantha, said Cribbs, turning back to Mrs. Swan, who was now stern-faced, *I'm glad to hear you're trying to talk some sense into young Jason.*

Pivoting back in my direction, Cribbs continued with a moralizing gaze. *You would do well to heed her advice.*

I nodded uncommittedly.

May I go to class? I asked, hoping to be freed from the awkward situation.

Go on, spat Cribbs, pointing absentmindedly toward the nearest hallway, and then continuing the conversation with Mrs. Swan.

As I sped toward the hall, I glanced back just in time for Mrs. Swan to look in my direction. Her face was impassive, but her eyes said *thank you*.

In the coming weeks, Mr. Albright and Mrs. Peyton separately confided in me their concern for my welfare and support for my stance, and both stressed the importance of secrecy, as they, too, would be ruined by the antiwhites if the truth about their concern for our people and culture were revealed.

Troublingly, they both echoed Mrs. Swan's warnings about the administration. And Mr. Albright also warned that he had overheard Cordell talking about fighting me away from the school. Apparently, Cordell didn't want any adults interfering with my beat-down.

Chapter 55

Counterstrike

Albright, Peyton, and Swan's support surprised and encouraged me. I wasn't alone, and that filled me with a sense of strength, fellowship, and deep gratitude, but the news about the administration's scheming drowned me in fearful speculations about what they were plotting, when they would strike, and what the fallout might be. But, after a day of worry, I realized that worrying was futile. I could only plan for so many possibilities. Beyond that, continuing to worry would paralyze me.

After contemplating steps I could take to shield myself from the administration, I turned my focus to Riddick and Cordell.

I knew I couldn't beat Riddick in a fight. If his skill, ferocity, strength, and size weren't enough, his gang members would jump me the moment I got the upper hand. What I needed was information. I needed to know everything I could about Riddick: where he lived, who his enemies were, if he had siblings, his class schedule, and where he hung out. I didn't know what I would do with the information, but I knew information was power: The more I knew about Riddick, the more choices I had.

By way of high school students from my neighborhood, I eagerly probed for details about my relentless hunter. I was surprised when information geysered my way like frothing champagne, but I shouldn't have been; Riddick had beaten up and terrorized so many kids that they couldn't wait to share what they knew.

In addition to finding out that he had two siblings at a local junior high, I discovered he had a criminal record and lived in public housing. I also learned a bit about his class schedule, his history, personality, and temperament, and where he hung out after school and on the weekends. The most important thing I learned was that he had an arch-enemy, Decker, a white senior who drove a colossal, mud-bogging truck, listened to country and heavy-metal music, wore skull-shaped rings with ferociously protruding spikes, and who had fought Riddick to a bloody draw the previous year.

With the info I gathered, I devised a plan to buy myself more time.

Riddick and his gang regularly searched the routes I took to and from school. Though I had avoided him by staying watchful and varying my travel times, I knew I couldn't avoid him forever. So I conspired with a high schooler to feed Riddick disinformation about the *reason* he had never seen me on my way home from school. The *reason*, as my high school confident informed a friend of Riddick's, was that I had been taking a meandering route to a relative's house in a different neighborhood, and from there I was driven home.

The route was nearly in the opposite direction of the routes I traveled. If the information reached Riddick, it would buy me the time I needed for the next step in my plan: to ally myself with Decker.

I sent messages to Decker through several kids who knew him. If he and I became friends, Riddick might back off. I'd be free of

Chapter 55 — Counterstrike

the terror that seized me every time I thought I saw the dirty Honda, free of the terror on those sleepless nights when I couldn't shake the panic of being attacked and blinded.

Having set my plans for Riddick in motion, I turned my attention to Cordell.

I didn't want to fight him; he was taller and much heavier than me. But as long as he plotted against me, I was in danger. I considered responding with an identical threat, but I instantly rejected the idea. The administration would surely be as intolerant of my efforts as they had been tolerant of his, as ready to punish me with smug indignation as they had excused him with permissive rationalizations.

I considered responding with bravado, boasting that I would have no problem beating him in a fight. But I rejected that idea as well: Mere words in response to his efforts would convey weakness.

I knew, then, what I had to do.

Despite my fears that I would be seriously hurt whether I won the fight or not, I had to fight him. After weighing my options, I decided to surprise Cordell on his way home from school: The administration wouldn't be able to punish me for the fight, and he wouldn't have a lynch mob with him.

As my plan depended on secrecy, I told no one, not even Adam or Chris. If Cordell found out, he would easily recruit the high school blacks who lived in his thuggish neighborhood to help him.

On a clement day a week later, I skipped the final period of school and ran home. Grabbing my bike, I rode hard for Cordell's

Crucible

neighborhood, a route that took me back by the school and miles in the opposite direction.

By the time I passed the school—keeping my distance in case Riddick was lying in wait—the final bell of the day had already rung: Cordell's bus was on its way.

As I feverishly rode, sweat lacquering my hair to my forehead and saturating my shirt, I was joined by a few small groups of kids who were cycling home. I told them what I was doing in the hope they would follow: If the blacks in Cordell's neighborhood lynched me for fighting him and wearing a Confederate flag, I wanted as many witnesses as possible.

As I approached the border of Cordell's neighborhood, I saw his bus sluggishly pulling away, belching black smoke from its tailpipe, its engine rattling noisily. He would be nearing home on foot. I had to hurry.

With a group of nearly ten eager onlookers strenuously racing to keep my pace, I zipped into the high-crime district, leaning my bike over to take the turn at speed, and pumping the pedals hard for the crest of the coming hill.

My lungs burning, my jacket flapping under my arms, the apex of the hill slowly dropped before me, and there he was: tall and broad-backed, walking down the far side of the hill with a gaggle of kids like little moons orbiting Jupiter.

Chapter 55 *Counterstrike*

I felt a rush of adrenalin. It was about to happen. I was about to fight Cordell, and then a realization hit me like a runaway car—I was totally exhausted: I had cycled for miles and had absolutely nothing left.

Overwhelmed by panic, the voice of fear conspired with logic to turn me around: *He hasn't seen me. I can turn around and go home and he'll never know I was here.*

NO—I have to fight him! I shouted back as my muscles trembled.

I can't win, though. I'm too tired to fight. I could skip a whole day of school next week and wait here for him, the voice frightfully pleaded.

NO! Do it now! Fight him again if I lose! I commanded myself.

And then, with a sharp glance over my shoulder, I realized the debate was pointless: There was a greedy audience of news propagators riding hard on my heels.

Turning back now, no matter how logical it seemed, was impossible.

Cordell! I roared, white-hot fire pumping fury through my veins.

He spun around, grimacing in perplexed rage at the harsh shout, squinting against the Sun's glare.

I stepped off my bike, letting it glide another 15 feet into someone's front yard before it toppled over. As I walked the remaining paces toward Cordell, my legs quivered with exhaustion.

The kids with Cordell scattered as though a grenade were tossed at their feet.

Are you ready mother-fucker? I demanded between gulps of air, the muscles in my chest, lats, and arms taut with anticipation, my fists balled and ready to strike with my next step—but his grimace suddenly broke.

Chapter 55   *Counterstrike*

    I halted, unsure of what to do, desperately trying to conceal my fatigue.

    Jason, he said in the sweetest voice a boy his size could muster, *you know we've always been friends.*

    What?! I shouted in my head, my chest heaving and a warm, wet sensation spreading over my frame: endorphins fighting my pain.

    What's he doing? Is he trying to trick me? Is he trying to get me to drop my guard? Cordell and I had only been friendly on a few occasions the previous year. We hadn't in any way "always been friends."

    What the hell are you talking about? I snarled, noticing my winded audience forming a half-moon around us, and the kids who had been with Cordell slowly inching back from their hasty retreat.

    You've told everybody how you're gonna kick my ass, chump—and you've been trying to get others to help you! So do it! Let's go!

    A brand new, diamond-silver Cadillac crawled by with a curious black woman at its helm, the Sun dancing on its gleaming wheels and our reflections gliding sinuously over its polished body.

    Yeah...I'm not anymore...I'm not...I know, no—listen, here's the thing, he said placatingly, taking small steps backward as he hitched his back-pack further up his shoulder and extended his hand pleadingly in front of him.

    Everybody's been talkin' stuff and I got caught up—you know. You know I never meant any of that shit, he finished on an upswing, shaking his head. *We're friends, man.*

Crucible

I didn't advance. The space between us continued to grow as he backed slowly away, a weak smile on his face.

We cool? he asked nervously.

Keeping my eyes on him, I retrieved my bike from what would have been a flowerbed before the neighborhood changed.

One more word about fighting me—

No! I won't. I promise, he said, placing his hand over his heart.

I glared at him, and then at the kids who were with him as if to say the warning applied to them as well.

Climbing on my bike, I nodded at Cordell, and then set off for home.

My bicycle-mounted audience showered me with adulation as we rode. I smiled stoically, unable to shake the image of the childlike fear I saw in Cordell's eyes: He was nothing but an empty swaggerer, a grandstander. I felt bad for the fright I caused him until I reflected on the fact that if he had successfully formed a lynch mob, they would have beaten me to a bloody mess. At least the silly fool would keep his mouth shut from here forward.

As my audience peeled off in ones and twos for home, I found myself traveling alone down one of the roads I had used to flee from Oakland and Adidas the previous year: I had changed—and I was changing my world, I thought to myself. I was doing what I was born to do.

Chapter 56

Gathering Storm

The news of my victory over Cordell spread through the school like wildfire in a kindling forest. Tales of fights and cowardly capitulations—such as Cordell's—had always excited wide curiosity, but this was different. The unimaginable had happened: A white kid had defied and prevailed against antiwhite violence.

Every day, kids privately told me about the fear and pain the Antiwhite Narrative caused them, their resentment of it, their secret opposition to it. Even kids I barely knew opened up to me, speaking softly with watchful eyes, thanking me for standing up for our people.

Now more than ever, my peers thanked me for helping them to see the Antiwhite Narrative for what it was—a raving hatred of white people and Western Civilization, underhandedly masqueraded as atonement for the "victim," and fanned by jealous mania for ill-gotten gains.

Adam and Chris, who had never truly abandoned me, spoke as openly with me as they had before my public stance. Even Mark and Kevin, and Greg and Ian cautiously talked to me again. But while I relished the revival in (mostly furtive) likability, the stares, the threatening *You'll soon get yours* glares from the antiwhite teachers and administrators increased.

While the antiwhite kids mutely watched in the hopeful expectancy that the administration would crush me for my heretical opinions, my friends and secret fans watched in helpless concern. I tried not to think about the administration. I had done all I could do to shield myself from them. My biggest concern was Decker—he hadn't responded to any of my messages. It seemed he had no interest in an alliance for the wellbeing of our people.

As each day ticked by like the apocalyptic second hand on a doomsday clock, my only smile was spurred by the sight of the unkempt Honda, swiftly gimping toward the false route like a fevered dung beetle rolling its meal: At least my disinformation had reached Riddick.

Two weeks after I defeated Cordell, Mrs. Swan stopped me short in the hall, tightly clutched my forearm and fixed me with a dark stare. *Be careful*, was all she muttered before continuing on her way as though she hadn't said a word, trilling at a teacher standing in the doorway of a classroom, *Having a pleasant day, Delores?*

As an approaching hurricane declares itself on the wind, in the taste it spills into the mouth and the sensation it washes over the body, everyone felt the antiwhite storm gathering in the form of Lamont Riddick and the school's administration: Riddick wouldn't search fruitlessly forever, ravenously circling my school like a shark in waters that lapped on the beaches of a shrinking island. He would eventually come through the doors to get me. And the administration gave every sign that it had accelerated its efforts to accomplish what intimidation and beat-downs had failed to accomplish: to silence, punish, and make an example of me.

Chapter 56 *Gathering Storm*

Everyone asked, *what will you do if Riddick comes in the school*...and, *what if the administration expels you*...and, *what if*...and, *what then*.... I didn't have answers. I knew only this: The last pieces on the chessboard were rapidly moving toward finality. For good or bad, the end was coming.

Chapter 57

Ancient Thunder

It had sounded like Cribbs said I was being expelled, but I must've been mistaken. I hadn't slept well the night before, worry-stricken about the administration and Riddick.

I had been summoned to Mr. Cribbs's office halfway through third period Monday morning. Cribbs and Wolf were seated there, and they both looked deadly serious.

Don't sit down, Cribbs coldly commanded. *We'll be heading over to Principal Stein's office in a moment.*

His chair bumped the wall, rattling framed certifications, as he brusquely left the room.

Principal Stein? I dimly repeated to myself, Wolf watching me with a calculating eye.

I never had a reason to see Stein. No one saw him unless they were being thrown out of school....

From a tire-screeching halt, my mind raced: *What's gonna happen to me? Are they really gonna expel me? What are my parents gonna say? Where will I go to school?*

Did Vice-principal Cribbs just say that I was being expelled? I asked shrinkingly, feeling a cool air chase the blood from my face.

We're starting the process. You've no one to blame but yourself, Wolf chided in a hard voice, looking deeply disapproving.

Chapter 57   *Ancient Thunder*

My knees suddenly felt weak and my throat went dry. It was over. I was finished. They had won.

Principal Stein may be willing to reconsider if you stop wearing that jacket and terrorizing your classmates, said Wolf reproachfully, rising from his chair.

Terrorizing my classmates? I echoed faintly.

He's ready, Cribbs said tersely from the doorway, a rancorous look punctuating his words as he sharply motioned for me to follow.

Run! my mind shouted fearfully. *Run as soon as I'm near the doors! Run!*

But I couldn't run. It wouldn't do me any good. They would just expel me in absentia.

With Cribbs in front and Wolf behind me, we wended toward Stein's office, nosily gawked at by the secretaries and the school nurse as though a whip's crack drove me to the gallows.

The spaciousness of Stein's office jarred me out of my anxious speculations.

Unlike Cribbs's dimly lit, island-malodorous bungalow, Stein's office was harshly bright and smelled of yellowing paper and the poignant ink on glossy magazines. His imposing, mahogany desk dominated the room like a baneful mountain range, glowering over the tightly-woven green-grey carpet, and serving as a headstone to all the unlucky ghosts who had sat before its judgment.

Three walls were dominated by disheveled bookshelves randomly stacked with books and periodicals, pagers and pocket knives, a pair of brass knuckles and the like. And the fourth wall—

made of one-way glass—looked creepily upon the main entrance to the school.

He's been in here staring at us, I heard my thought chillingly say.

From the top of the desk, a book's red title leapt blaringly into view: *Diversity Training and Overcoming Resistance*. And then another: *The Youth and Inculcating Multicultural Values*. And then another: *Discipline*.

A grim man sat behind the desk. He was sickly-thin and greasily capped by a furious comb-over. His eyes loomed menacingly behind wire-rimmed spectacles, and his pointed, gaunt face clung unnaturally to his feeble neck.

It was Stein.

A faux spider plant hung from the ceiling behind him, its leaves covered in a thick layer of dust, and my mother was sitting— MY MOTHER?!

My inner voice choked on the sight of her. She was stiffly seated across from Stein, incredulously glaring at me, as severe as I had ever seen her.

Take a seat, Jason, invited Stein, leering at me with deepest loathing, the red book titles sliding reflectively across the lenses of his glasses.

I joined my mother across from Principal Stein. Painfully conscious of the displeasure radiating from her like heat from boiling water, I avoided her eyes.

Chapter 57   *Ancient Thunder*

Cribbs flopped down on a threadbare, dark orange, county-issued sofa, and watched me with a mixture of anger and satisfaction on his face. Wolf circled around behind Stein, leaned against the bookshelf and disinterestedly examined an ancient knife he pulled from the shelf.

Do you know why you're here—Jason? asked Stein in a disdainful air.

No, I responded hollowly.

Cribbs suppressed a guffaw, rolled his eyes, folded and unfolded his arms.

I find that hard to believe, sneered Stein, examining me over his glasses.

Why are you here? he repeated, a thin edge to his voice, clearly commanding me to speak.

My jacket, I answered him, scarcely willing to talk.

That's part of it. Can you think of nothing else? he mercilessly goaded.

As quick as the blink of an eye, a grin fleeted over his face. That bastard was enjoying this.

No, I answered firmly, a flame jumping to life amid the desolate cold of my fears, threatening to ignite my anger.

What about the fights you've been in?

I've only defended myself—Principal Stein.

Stein chuckled. *That's not what I've gathered.*

He peered over at Wolf, brushed back a few clumps of his comb-over that had fallen hideously over his face, and continued.

Isn't it true you attempted to fight Cordell the other day because he's black?

No! I spat, sitting forward in my chair.

Jason! reproached my mother, but I couldn't have cared less. At that moment, I confirmed—as though realizing it all over again—

Chapter 57   *Ancient Thunder*

that Stein, Wolf, and Cribbs were not impartial, they were the enemy. They were not adults or authority figures deserving respect, they were merciless barbarians deserving no mercy, pitiless monsters deserving no pity. They were destroyers of my civilization, and I was a defender at the gates.

If my mother objected to my stand, then I would have no mother! There was no more time for sentimentality, no more time for pacification of the enemy and our weakest, most craven members—it was time to stand.

With a raised voice, I responded, *Cordell's been trying to get a group of kids to fight me all year! I told you all that—I've been telling you all about kids threatening and attacking me all this year and last! And yeah. I tried to fight Cordell because of what he was trying to do—not because he's black, and I let him off the hook when he said he didn't mean it—*

Psh—it's more likely you took off when you saw adults witnessing what you were about to do, interrupted Cribbs, folding his arms and shaking his head disbelievingly.

That's not true!

Jason, shot Stein, drawing my attention from Cribbs, *even if that's not true, what about all your other attacks on minorities?*

Attacks?! They've attacked me and I've defended myself. Have you not been listening?!

So the world's out to get you, Jason? asked Wolf with a mocking tongue and stupid grin, still fiddling with the knife.

225

This school needs to protect my son if he's being attacked, my mother injected in a submissive tone.

Raising a mollifying hand in her direction, Stein said, *I can assure you, Mrs. Köhne, Jason has not been attacked and he's in no danger whatsoever—aside from the danger he creates for himself, of course.*

That's a lie! I growled.

Don't get excited, Jason—I don't intimidate as easily as your peers, Stein replied, his beady leer glittering venomously.

I held his gaze, refusing to submit, refusing to be intimidated by the antiwhite pigs anymore. As we glared at each other, I could have sworn I saw a flash of something in his eyes, a darkness with ancient roots.

Just like the others, he wasn't concerned with inclusion, diversity, sensitivity, or any of the other catchwords and catchphrases the antiwhites use to lull the ignorant and unwary: For him, they were just pretexts—tools for the erasure of whites from our Western Civilization.

He finally broke my gaze and continued silkily.

We've also the matter to discuss about you threatening to fight everyone who disagrees with you.

I haven't said I'd fight anybody who disagrees with me! I've only said I would treat everyone who tries to get me jumped as though they were jumping me.

Chapter 57 Ancient Thunder

So you admit you'd attack those who "get you jumped"—as you say? grinned Stein. *And what about all your racist language in class and with your peers?*

My mother shifted nervously at the word—racist.

Now, I know Jason has a lot of opinions, but I don't believe he's said anything truly racist, said my mother, shaking her head skeptically.

I'm not sure what Jason has been telling you, Mrs. Köhne, but I'm afraid Jason is known for saying things that cross the line, disagreed Wolf in an apologetic tone, as though he were breaking the news of a family death.

Jason! Is that true? demanded my mother, turning to me with the trained look of horror that we had seen portrayed by parents in similar situations on television and in the movies.

They call everything racist that isn't antiwhite, I answered her flatly.

That's another serious problem, Mrs. Köhne—Jason has an unhealthy fixation on a delusion that society is out to get white people, said Stein with an oily expression of smug complacence. *Have you had him evaluated for psychiatric problems?*

Wolf grinned and nodded to himself, as though impressed by Stein's line of questioning.

No, answered my mother in a worried tone, pinching her hands between her knees.

Perhaps you should, said Stein. *Have you had him tested for drug use?*

No, but Jason wouldn't use drugs.

His behavior is abnormal, and he has some significant bags under his eyes—

That's because I can't sleep for the worry about you people! I spat, causing my mother to flinch.

Stein looked at me as though I were a bug he was studying, and then turned back to my mother. *It might also be prudent to have him tested for drug use. We often see drug use and psychiatric problems in antisocial boys like Jason. Perhaps he should be medicated—*

I'm not antisocial, I broke in, in total shock at another baseless accusation.

I told Jason this jacket would get him into trouble, said my mother, *but I don't think he's antisocial. He has a lot of friends and participates in sports and Boy Scouts year round. If we can get him to stop wearing this jacket to school, can we forego expulsion?*

Stein tilted his head as though considering her request.

It goes a lot deeper than his jacket, hotly interrupted Cribbs. *He's influencing his peers with hate speech—and intimidating minorities… Jim Crow is dead.*

Stein nodded agreement as though something profound had just been said.

My mother continued. *He would obviously have to stop all that—*

I think it would demonstrate real commitment on Jason's part if he rescinded the hurtful and offensive things he's said—and

Chapter 57 — Ancient Thunder

apologized to all of us and to everyone he's frightened with his statements, advised Wolf, cutting off my mother, to which she nodded acquiescently, her stare sailing from Wolf and docking on me.

I'm not gonna stop wearing my jacket, I responded adamantly. *You let the black kids wear their Malcolm X shirts.*

They're celebrating black pride and culture, Cribbs roared dismissively with his passive-aggressive smile.

And I'm celebrating white pride and culture!

You mean white supremacism! countered Cribbs.

I'll never take it off, I growled, daring Cribbs with a hard stare to try and force me.

My mother turned red, glaring at me as Cribbs continued.

This is the kind of insolence we've had to deal with for the past year and a half. How do we know Jason hasn't been burning crosses in people's yards?

What?! Are you serious?! I said, in shock.

Absolutely...that's what—

Have there been any reports of cross burnings? I cut in.

How do we know the victims aren't too afraid to report it? I'm sure the last thing they want are Nazis and Klansmen storming their houses in retaliation, ludicrously retorted Cribbs, his arms outstretched in soliciting support as he exchanged nodding agreement with Stein and Wolf. *How do we know Jason hasn't been destroying school property to get back at the system he delusionally considers opposed to whites and Western Civilization—*

Crucible

I know Jason has expressed unpopular opinions, but I'm certain he wouldn't do any of that, said my mother disbelievingly.

This goes well beyond unpopular opinions, Mrs. Köhne, Stein scathingly interrupted. *Jason has engaged in hate speech. He wears a symbol of hate, and he has oppressed and intimidated minorities with violence. He's disliked by most if not all of his peers because of his virulent racism and bigotry, and he's a continuing disruption to the purpose of this school.*

There was a long silence. Stein sniffed deeply and ran a hand across his forehead, brushing back another clump of greasy hair.

The three antiwhite pigs hadn't realized it, but something had changed in the room, some new energy seethed with volcanic intensity. In their antiwhite haste to destroy a defender at the gates of white, Western Civilization, they had crossed an ancient and terrible line, a line sewn deeply into genetic memory: a mother's defense of her young.

Bristling at his words, my mother responded, *You all seem to be ganging up on Jason.*

Without moving his head, Cribbs's white eyes jumped across his black face and landed on Stein.

We are doing no such thing, exploded Stein with a sneer. *We're trying to remedy disruptive behavior. If we cannot count on your help, Mrs. Köhne, then we will proceed with expulsion.*

That did it. Now she was really mad.

If you think you're going to push me around like you push students around, you've got another goddamned thing coming, she shouted, pointing an angry finger across the desk. *Jason says that black kids are allowed to wear Malcolm X shirts. Unless you ban their pride, you can't ban his!*

Mrs. Köhne—growled Stein as a purple vein came to life on his temple, throbbing through his pasty skin, but my mother cut him off.

You take one step to expel Jason, and I'll sue the county.

Now, let's just calm down, said Wolf placatingly. *There's no use in getting upset—and there's no use in suing city hall, as they say.*

Oh, I don't care if I lose, because I'll also sue the hell out of the three of you for harassment and anything else a lawyer can dream up.

The antiwhite pigs' pompous, self-assured, commanding persona fled from the office with its tale between its legs.

Stein, Wolf, and Cribbs hemmed and hawed as my mother blasted into a litany of county, state, and federal institutions she could seek assistance from in the defense of her son, and from which she could solicit decisive action.

I've heard enough, blubbered Stein, getting clumsily to his feet, long greasy strings of his comb-over falling wildly across his face, giving him a crazed, bedraggled appearance.

Mark my words, hotly warned my mother as we left the office, *you take any action against my son, and today won't be the last you hear from me!*

Crucible

Like a zombie, I plodded from one class to the next for the rest of the day, stunned by the possibility of expulsion, my mother's sudden willingness to go to war on my behalf, and fearful of what shape the fight with the school might take.

Would there be lawyers and lawsuits? Would county, state, and federal institutions be marshaled? If it hadn't been for the news I received from high schoolers in my neighborhood, I might have been numb for weeks. But my entire body and mind had been electrifyingly jolted to life with a painful urgency: Riddick was coming for me. Tired of searching, he said he would enter my school on the coming Friday, *blind the racist,* and *burn his jacket.*

Chapter 58

Damned Either Way

Jeopardizing the tenuous peace I had won for myself, Riddick had also sent word that he backed all the antiwhites in my school. His message included a threat to anyone who sided or agreed with me, saying he would beat them down as well.

What are you gonna do? asked Adam amid the theater's twilit despair.

The bell signaling the end of the most agonizing Tuesday in my life had rung twenty minutes earlier, its unbodied echo arcing through my mind as a death knell frenziedly rung by Stein and Riddick.

I wearily raised my head from where I hung it over my lap on the edge of the stage, looked blankly at Adam and Chris seated in the second row, and then dropped it again without saying a word.

What do you think Principal Stein is gonna do? added Chris worriedly.

I guess he'll expel me, and then there'll be a huge legal battle, I mumbled, still examining my lap. *My parents don't have a lot of money, and I can promise there won't be multi-million-dollar organizations elbowing each other out of the way to come to my aid—like the antiwhites always have. And there won't be governmental agencies trampling over each other as they race to my defense—like the antiwhites always have. And there won't be media empires striving*

Crucible

to outdo each other with stories about my persecution—(Chris commiseratingly chorused with me) *like the antiwhites always have.*

If the media say anything, it'll be about how you need to be expelled and locked up, Chris guffawed, throwing his hands in the air exasperatedly. *Shit, if reporters come here, they'd ask the kids who jumped you what it's like to be a victim of hate and intolerance.*

Yeah, yeah, and they'd ask Jason what it's like to be prejudiced. And then they'd ask what happened in his past that made him so intolerant, predicted Adam bitterly, mocking the media's pretexts of impartiality and fairness.

Maybe you should just run away, suggested Chris, half seriously. *Then your parents won't have the legal expenses, and you won't have to worry about Riddick.*

I shook my head ruefully. *No. I can't run. I've got nowhere to go, and if I run now, I'll be running from the Steins and Riddicks of the world for the rest of my life. At least I know what my parents will do about Stein if he expels me. But other than your suggestion that I bring a knife to school on Friday* (I looked dejectedly at Chris), *I don't know what I'm gonna do about Riddick.*

I initially balked at the idea of pulling a knife for fear that stabbing Riddick would get me arrested, even though it would be self-defense (the antiwhites would go berserk about an unashamed white kid stabbing a nonwhite, regardless of the circumstances), but imprisonment and keeping my eyesight sounded a lot better than being blinded.

Chapter 58 *Damned Either Way*

There was a slim chance that I might not have to stab him, though. I had been given two butterfly knives by a high school kid the previous year, and for fun I had taught myself to use them like a martial arts master: one at a time—passing it back and forth between hands, and even two at a time—one in each hand.

Maybe seeing the flourish of the gleaming blades as I drew them from my pockets would be enough to scare Riddick and his gang. But then again, they were knives, and knives were prohibited in school. My parents wouldn't have a chance in hell of preventing my expulsion if I were caught with butterfly knives.

I contemplated bringing one or both pairs of my nunchucks. I had bartered for them with a different high schooler over the summer, and like the butterfly knives, I had (painfully) taught myself to use them like Chuck Norris: one at a time, and even both pairs at once. I hadn't heard any rules about nunchucks. But then again, they seemed deadlier than butterfly knives, and the punishment likely sterner.

Twirling his finger absentmindedly as though paging through his memory, Adam asked, *Whatever happened to that high schooler? Why won't he help you?*

Decker? (Adam nodded, *Yeah.*) *I don't know. I guess, like most whites, he doesn't care about our wellbeing. He's just a rebel without a cause—and a people.*

Looks like you're out of options, bemoaned Chris. *I think you should just bring the knives—I wouldn't let that thug blind me.*

I nodded ambivalently.

Crucible

I wanted to—I really wanted to bring the butterfly knives. Part of me loved the idea of amazed terror on Riddick's face as the knives menacingly rung with blinding speed over my hands, glistening sharply with a deadly thirst in the school's florescent lights.

He had terrorized me for so long…. But when I thought about the repercussions (expulsion, arrest, imprisonment, rape in a prison cell, lying vilification at the hands of a pompously self-righteous, antiwhite Regime), I shrank away from the fantasy, tucking myself into the darkest corner of my mind: alone, frightened, hiding.

Stein will expel me any day now, and Riddick will come for me on Friday, I thought heavily to myself, *either way, it'll soon be over.*

Chapter 59

Clarity

There was a palpable energy in the air by Wednesday morning. Everyone in the school knew I was on the verge of expulsion, and everyone knew Riddick was coming for me on Friday. The antiwhite kids were giddy with excitement.

Their daily murmurs against me had returned to open declarations. They were leering at me, simpering at me, laughing at me. They received the news of my approaching beat-down with a sick festivity. Their antiwhite faith called them to that. It called them to blindly destroy the West and to celebrate its destruction as passage to the "nirvana" of places like the Soviet Union and communist China.

I was shocked at how quickly they transformed from spineless, groveling, talentless nothings, to prigs: brash, taunting, self-styled dictators of social protocol—unwashed, invisible, and ingratiating one day; self-righteous, vicious, and contemptuous the next.

As I absent-mindedly wended to my final class of the day, I abruptly realized with a flinch of horror that Riddick was going to be armed when he came for me: He was going to bring something to gouge my eyes out.

My stomach trembled nauseatingly and my head swam. I stepped out of the path of traffic and leaned against a fire extinguisher for support.

Crucible

Resting there unsteadily, I nervously raced over my options: Tell the administration? No. They won't believe me or care. Tell the police? No. They won't care about a kid wearing a Confederate flag, except maybe to investigate me. Tell my parents and add to the trouble I'm already causing them. No. They can't protect me from Riddick forever. Bring my butterfly knives or nunchucks to defend myself? No. Every scenario involving weapons resulted in bad to horrific consequences.

There was really only one thing I could do—the one thing I'd been dismissing as far too bold, far too dangerous—

Jason, said Mr. Albright's voice, jarring me out of my tangled contemplation.

He emerged from the thinning crowd in the hall and waited for a few curious kids to pass before continuing in a dropped voice.

They're not going to expel you. They made the decision this afternoon. Apparently, they were none too pleased with the prospect of lawsuits after talking with a county attorney.

I stared at him disbelievingly, unable to question or thank him for the news.

Mind yourself, though, he finished, leaning in. *They'll use any excuse to expel you.*

He disappeared around the corner, and just like that, the dark threat of imminent expulsion was gone.

The bell signaling the start of the day's final period rang me into the silence of the deserted hall. I stood motionless for several minutes, assimilating Albright's news.

Chapter 59   *Clarity*

All that was left was for me to do my part.

Tomorrow, I bravely said to myself, thrusting my weight back onto my feet and curling my fingers into a fist, *a day before Riddick comes for me, I'll take the fight to him!*

Chapter 60

Into the Monster's Den

Most of the information I had gathered on Riddick was useless, but one piece opened the door to my plan: I knew exactly where he would be just before his lunch. He had planned to attack me at my school; he would never expect me to come for him at his.

At 11:00 on Thursday morning, I scrambled from an unfrequented backdoor near the gym, furtively ambled behind a copse, over a fence, and down a sloping hill until I reached the road, out of sight—and hopefully out of the minds—of my teachers and the administration.

My nerves were a fraying rope, spun so tightly there was no room for air, and under such a load that the breaking strands sang like an executioner's axe drawn from a whetstone. More than a half mile of busy roadway stretched dauntingly between me and the high school. Someone would see me: a police officer, a staffer from either school, a concerned parent, a security guard—the enormous high school had a small but zealous contingent of security guards. And my Confederate jacket would surely get me noticed.

I pulled it off and slung it under my arm as I took my first, hesitant step.

I was anxious. I concentrated on my feet—one foot in front of the other—one in front of the other. *Keep walking*, I told myself. *Keep my head down.*

Chapter 60   *Into the Monster's Den*

The continual thrum of tires over pavement tore me from my focus.

Ignore it, I said adamantly.

Some vehicles slowed as they passed.

Ignore it! I ordered.

The hum of the gasoline engines contrasted with the rattle of the diesels.

Ignore it!

The drivers are looking at me. I'm the only one out here. They know I should be in school, persisted a voice in my head. *They know!*

Dammit! Ignore it!

The swinging pitch as cars neared and then flew away spoke with an incessant murmur: *Somebody's gonna see you. They're looking at you. You're gonna get caught.*

Focus! I commanded myself.

What if somebody stops? a voice in my head fearfully asked, thrusting my senses into a painful acuity.

I'll run where they can't follow. They won't know who I am, I answered the insistent voice. *Just keep walking.*

As I plodded, every part of my body rebelled. My wrist, sore from pull-ups, began to ache. My elbow, tender from pushups, began to throb. The cadence of my breath fluctuated painfully: short, choppy gulps; long gasps. My lips tingled, and my tongue went dry.

Go back to school! pleaded the voice.

Stop it!

Run home! defiantly begged the voice.

No! Keep going! I angrily ordered.

Every step felt heavier, more burdensome than the last, more torturous than the one before, but finally, like the ebbing sting of a slap to the skin, the voice abated.

I was numb. The road clamor drifted away. I dissolved into the melody of my shoes striking the sidewalk and the tempered rhythm of the air passing through my lungs.

I lost time. I didn't know how long I had been walking, but the moment I wondered how much farther I had to go—a forbidding, stone giant arose before me: Colossal compared to my junior high, the high school drew into view like a menacing fortress, an enemy citadel housing a labyrinthian network of unfamiliar halls and stairwells, throngs of strangers, students, teachers, guards, and administrators.

Who is he? they were likely to ask themselves. *Where are you from? What are you doing here, young man?*

What's your name? they would likely demand. *Come with me,* they were likely to order.

Somewhere behind the lofty walls and maze of dangers that awaited me was the sophomore cafeteria, and in the cafeteria was the sophomore commons, where I would find my hunter.

I'll need to ask some kids where to go, I abruptly thought.

They'll tell on you, the voice spoke up, weaker than before.

It won't matter if they do. It'll be over by the time—I'm caught....

The truth hit me hard in the gut—the truth I had refused to acknowledge: I'll probably get caught, and if I'm caught, I'll be expelled. And worse, I'll probably lose the fight and get severely injured as well.

Under the high school's glowering shadow, I had stopped walking without realizing it.

I can't beat the antiwhites alone. I'm just a kid against the schools and administrations, and multi-million-dollar organizations, and police, and government, and media.

Hopelessness rooted me to the concrete, dragging down my face, my heart, my spirit, but a winged idea sped through me, branching and growing as I gave it attention: I live only once. My life is mine to give as I see fit.

Others might choose to make their lives worthless, partying and pursuing useless hobbies and idle distractions, but I choose to make my life a treasure; I choose to give my life to the greatest of all causes, to the wellbeing of the people who are the soul of the West, who have raised the world with their genius and labors from darkness to light. If it's within me, the future Shakespeares, Beethovens, Pasteurs, and Newtons, and the future Edisons, Jacksons, Bacons, and Aristotles, and the future Westmen who'll take us to the moons of Saturn, Jupiter, and beyond, they will live because I was one of the Westmen who gave his life to the cause of our wellbeing.

At that moment, I sacrificially laid my life on the altar of the West. Breaking free of my lingering fears, I confidently headed into the high school, pulling on my Confederate jacket as I went.

Chapter 61

The Spirit of the West

The bell rang portentously when I walked through the doors. Instantly, students spilled from all directions, riding a raucous wave that drowned the spacious lobby and its radial halls from floor to ceiling.

Kids cascaded down broad steps to my left and funneled into the swelling expanse, breaking into disjointed streams heading this way and that. Most of them were bigger than me, and their bustle and noise easily exceeded the like at my junior high. I was disoriented and unnoticed.

A pretty blonde in a contour-flattering red skirt caught my eye as she passed. I raised my hand beseechingly and said, *Can you tell me where I can find the sophomore commons?*

She gave me a queer look, but chimed, *Sure. You take that hall over there. Follow it until you reach your first left. Go down that hall and you'll see the sophomore commons on your left.*

Okay, thanks, I nervously smiled.

As soon as I stepped into the crowd, I heard what I'd been dreading: *Look at dat boy's jacket*, cackled a black female's sinister voice from the jumble of bodies and sounds that surrounded me.

Oh my gawd, oh my gawd, cried another.

You see dat shit!

I refused to acknowledge them.

Chapter 61   *The Spirit of the West*

    Single-mindedly forcing myself through the book-bag-laden, jostling crowd, I entered the first hall, and there were fresh words at my back.

    Look at his jacket, said a white boy's surprised voice.

    Sweet Jesus, he's gonna get killed, a second voice answered the first.

    A burly white boy in a Guns N' Roses t-shirt and white high-top sneakers loped heavily up beside me.

    Hey, do you go to school here? he asked with a note of interest, a venerational look on his square face.

    No. I'm just here for 10 minutes, I responded flatly, glancing at him as I continued to cut through the congestion.

    I turned the final corner just ahead of an Asian boy struggling on crutches, and stepped up the pace.

    That motha-fucka gotta be lost, satirically bayed a black boy's voice from behind me, followed by a pother of derisive laughter.

    Ignore them, I said to myself. *I'm almost there.*

    A moment later, I drew near and stepped through a set of large doors, and there it was—er, or there they were....

    Sweeping banks of red lockers sprang like rows of corn into view on my left, but just a little further along—also on my left—were sweeping banks of green lockers. Both red and green locker commons joined separate cafeterias.

    Where are the sophomores? a panicked voice suddenly piped in my head, as high schoolers callously pushed past me.

Excuse me, I approached a white boy with livid razor burn on his throat and the biggest Adam's apple I'd ever seen.

How many colors of lockers are there?

Four, he supplied, *red, green, black, and white.*

Four colors, I bewilderedly repeated.

The black and white ones are on the other side of the school—they're for juniors and seniors, he continued.

Which ones are for sophomores, I quickly implored.

Red.

Thanks, man.

Anytime, he shot back, and he headed through the doors behind me, adjusting his glasses.

I threw my attention at the red lockers as an adult's voice madly yelled from somewhere off to my right. I backed against the wall and whipped my head toward the shout. A black man, obviously one of the security guards, was scolding kids I couldn't see.

He'd been walking in my direction when whatever it was had caught his attention, and he was poised to continue toward me.

If he comes this way, I'll be caught! a thought gasped.

I frantically searched for somewhere to hide. There was a door a few yards to my right.

I'll slide in there if he comes—say I'm lost if someone's inside.

No! They'll know I don't belong here, shouted my inner voice as my heart pounded in my ears.

He's coming! Go!

I slid along the wall toward the door, grabbed the handle—

Chapter 61 The Spirit of the West

Wait....

His walky-talky held to his head, he abruptly turned and set off in the other direction, emphatically answering the call as he fell into a jog, a ring of keys jingling wildly on his hip through the hum of voices.

I've got to hurry.

I pulled away from the door and surveyed the whirlwind of students, some standing at their lockers, some passing through the area, some already with their lunches and sitting down at large round tables: There were boys well over six feet tall and girls with women's bodies; there were clean-cut kids and uncouth cliquish-loners dressed like underworld characters from low-budget films; there were robust athletes and emaciated nerds and loud kids and quiet kids.... How would I ever find—

My eyes had sped over him twice before I realized I was looking at Riddick. He was leaning against the first row of lockers, directly across from where I watched him, camouflaged by the chaos of kids crisscrossing in front of me. The dybbuk's monster, the one Adam had prophetically warned me about when I resolved to challenge the Regime's Antiwhite Narrative, couldn't be more than twenty feet away.

The self-styled "champion of *minority* rights" was talking to another black kid. They were dressed like thugs, and everyone who passed yielded them a wide berth. From previous sightings, I knew he was taller and burlier, but at four years older than me, standing this close made his advantages look even more pronounced. He blinked into and out of view as kids passed between us. His face was cruel; his eyes simmered with hatred and violence under a low brow and close-cropped hair.

Several white boys cravenly cast their gaze to the floor as he leered at them while they scurried by, and yet, a moment later, he lustfully gawked after pretty white girls sashaying in the other direction, licking his lips as they passed.

I took a slow, deep breath. *No more delaying. No more excuses,* I muttered to myself. *Now for war—now for vengeance—now for the West.*

As though out of respect for the gravity of the final act, fate parted the curtain of bodies before me. Setting my jaw, I steeled my resolve, leapt forward at a run through the gap in the crowd—all my fury, all my might, my fist drawn back, and I blasted Lamont Riddick in the face!

The world ran red, and tore into alternating snippets of fast and slow motion, roaring sound, and abrupt silence.

He had spotted me at the last moment and jerked his head, saving himself from the full impact of the blow, but I wasn't finished.

As soon as my right had landed, I fired my left. His head violently popped sideways and he shoved me back.

I lunged forward: a glancing right to his face—left to his stomach—right to his ribs, left cross to his jaw. I was giving him everything I had—my strength, my speed, my revenge.

Don't let him recover! a voice shouted in my head.

Chapter 61 *The Spirit of the West*

He leaned forward, ducking his head between his arms and shoved me hard, sending me stumbling backward, which bought him the space he needed.

Reddened from the blows, his face twisted with rage. The element of surprise was gone. The fight was on.

You recognize me, mother-fucker! I shouted as kids gushed into a ring around us, scrambling up lockers and climbing on tables for a better view, zestfully shouting, *FIGHT!*

I'm gonna kill you, racist bitch! he roared wickedly.

It was the first time I heard him speak, but his voice seemed terrifyingly reminiscent of his specter in my nightmares.

I ran forward and smashed him into the lockers, backpedaling out of his reach as he wildly grabbed at me with heavy paws.

Is that all you got, punk bitch?! he mockingly spat, dropping his fists as though unconcerned, and then drawing them up again, ready to fight.

Riddick's friend, pointing at me and gawking searchingly at the crowd, bellowed astonishedly, *That's the racist! That's the fucking racist we after!*

Like a boxer, Riddick bounced on his toes toward me, his thick forearms and bulbous fists tucked tightly to his body and face. Driven by bloodlust, the crowd heckled and hounded us to ravage each other: *Hit him! Knock him out! Kick his ass! Don't be a pussy!*

I drove in, feigning like I was going right, but throwing my left. He backpedaled, blocked and threw a wild right that whipped by my mouth with enough force to knock my teeth out.

Crucible

Don't let him hit you! a fearful voice cried in my head.

I planted my back foot, dashed forward with my head down, collided with his chest, and drove him crashingly into the lockers, rattling the row, causing kids perched atop to lose their balance and fall to the floor.

A hoarse cheer rose from the exuberant crowd.

I threw a glancing right to his face, another with my left, and a hard right to his ribs. He shoved me back and landed a devastating blow to my jaw.

I was staggered. The floor tipped dangerously to the right and then to the left.

He bounded forward—I covered up.

Punch after punch smashed into my head, my ears, my forearms—crunching sounds joining the blows—*Were bones breaking? Was cartilage tearing?*

I fired an uppercut between the impacts—my knuckles bashing his mouth, backing him off, blood fountaining from his lips.

The soft tissue had been horribly split against his crooked teeth, which now, painted crimson with gore, gave him the appearance of a wild animal feasting on a corpse.

OH MY GOD! screamed a girl somewhere to my right as Riddick searched his mouth with his fingers, and then bellowed incoherently, baring his blood-soaked teeth in rage.

He charged—I threw a jab he took to the chin—he seized and vaulted me through the air, sending me stumbling and then sliding

Chapter 61 *The Spirit of the West*

along the floor, past the end of the locker rows and toward the lunch tables, caroming off the legs of kids trying to get out of the way.

The crowd was screaming and running, knocking into and over each other to make room for the fight as Riddick came for me.

Halfway to my feet, his fingers sank into my jacket, and he hurled me into the end of a row of lockers, my head hammering the unforgiving sheet metal. I swayed on feet, my ears rang, and tiny iridescent stars zipped through my vision.

Growling, he came at me with a mouthful of bloody teeth.

Crucible

As I edged to my right along the end of the locker rows, I spotted a large trashcan. I tipped it between us—he stumbled against it—kicking it—I attacked, landing a left jab and then a grazing right cross to his face; gooey ropes of blood slung from his mouth, splashing the lockers and the white tile floor at his feet.

He leapt forward, throwing roundhouses as I backpedaled along the locker rows, dodging his punches until one annihilatingly caught me on the cheek.

The acrid taste and odor of blood flooded my senses.

Are my teeth broken? a horrified voice screamed in my head as I spit something small and red to the floor—I had bitten off a piece of my tongue.

I covered up. He threw a hard left to my ribs that lifted me off the ground, agonizingly forcing the air from my lungs. Jagged bolts of pain shot around my back and across my stomach.

I shoved him and staggered backward, the locker rows and aisles alternating to my left.

My hip?! a panicked voice cried in response to pain that radiated from the joint.

I couldn't breathe. My cheek was getting heavy and thick. My ribs were ablaze with pain, and Riddick was still coming, growling, his chest heaving, and his chin smeared with gore.

I can't fight anymore, a voice screamed. *I can't beat him. Just stop! Just give up!*

The reality that it was over sunk deep roots into me. He was going to win and I knew it.

Chapter 61   *The Spirit of the West*

Another step backward and I saw a tall stack of papers atop the lockers beside me. I swept them at Riddick and they exploded in a great shower as he swatted at them disorientedly.

Wanting to use the diversion to run for my life, I mechanically advanced, throwing a right that finally landed hard on his face, briefly staggering him.

I followed with a tired left, still unable to draw a full breath. He blocked it and grabbed me. Grunting, he launched me with all his might into the air. I stumbled and crashed wildly through a lunch table and chairs: wood and metal, trays and food, sodas and hard plastic seats skipped through my vision, my head bouncing off the tile floor when I came to rest.

I was gulping for air, finally able to breathe, but it was over.

Stay down! my inner voice paralyzingly commanded, as a dozen new points of agony assailed my thoughts from all over my body.

I raised my head. My vision in my left eye was blurry and the lid felt hot. Something was crawling down my neck. I grabbed at it and looked at my fingers; they were dipped with blood. My earlobe was torn and bleeding.

Stay down! the voice ordered again. *All right. All right—I can't do this.*

Riddick glowered from 10 feet away, panting heavily. *GET UP! Get up and get some more motha-fucka!*

He coughed, swallowed hard, and choked on his uncontrolled gasps. *Dat jacket's mine!*

Don't let him take my jacket! I reflexively shouted in my head. *But I can't—I can't stop him. He's too big—nothing hurts him.*

The weight of my powerlessness eclipsed the pain of my injuries with grief. He was going to take my jacket and destroy my flag. He was going to humiliate me in front of everyone, and there was nothing I could do to stop him.

The news would reach my school. The antiwhites would mock and laugh at me. The teachers and administration would grin knowingly—and then they would expel me. Their destruction of my people and Western Culture would continue—another victory on their road to our obliteration.

My thoughts vainly scrambled back in time over my decisions. Where had I gone wrong? How had it come to this? The searing flash of instant regret was unbearable. Unexpectedly, I saw my jacket in my mind's eye, my hand clutching the blazing flag. But it wasn't sadness that filled me at that moment; it was an odd stillness and peace—a quiet that harbored a quickening pulse.

If faith and fire was all I ever had, I suddenly knew it was all I ever needed.

I rose angrily to my feet as Riddick arrogantly spat through heavy gasps, *Wuss up, bitch—you ready to quit?*

As soon as I win.

A trace of fear swept through Riddick's exhausted eyes—and I charged!

He backpedaled, blocking and covering up as I launched punch after punch at his face and ribs with renewed ferocity, some of

Chapter 61 — The Spirit of the West

the blows hitting their mark, but most landing vainly against his thick forearms.

It wasn't going to be enough. I had to do something else.

I shot my hands between his fists, grabbed both sides of his head, and I slammed my forehead into his face with all my might.

He broke away with a guttural howl of pain, sliding to his right into one of the aisles, leaning his back against the lockers for support.

His left arm futilely extended in blind defense as he groped at his injuries with his right, I chased him into the aisle, swatted his left arm aside and landed an explosive right to his face. He staggered further, sliding further down the aisle, his eyes rolling. I drew back, and launched another hard right to his face. He stumbled further—I planted my left foot, threw a heavy left hook that slammed into his jaw with a sickening pop, arresting his slide, standing him upright, his arms swatting blindly at space, his head wobbling on his shoulders. I drew back my right, swiveled my hips, rotating on the balls of my feet—everything I had—and BLASTED him in the face.

Consciousness darted from his dark eyes. His knees buckled and his arms fell slack to his sides, and Lamont Riddick, the dybbuk's monster, crumpled to the floor.

The crowd was shouting as I stared down at him, my fingers painfully curled into fists and my chest heaving under my chin. I raised my eyes to a mêlée: kids running in all directions, chairs, tables, and trashcans shoved pell-mell out of the way.

What's going on? I asked as I fearfully scuttled up the aisle.

SECURITY! my mind screamed as I realized what they were shouting.

I launched myself into a run, dodging kids as I scampered through the crowd, adrenaline pushing me far beyond my fatigue and injuries. No idea where I was going, I emerged in a hall, took a left and opened my stride to a sprint.

Chapter 61   *The Spirit of the West*

The crowd and its noise subsided as I blindly rocketed down another hall. A moment later, I burst into an expanse with halls branching in several directions—it was the lobby! Turning right, I blasted through the high school's front doors.

Chapter 62

Western Sunrise

Before the end of the following week, the news of my impossible victory over Riddick had spread throughout my school. My friends were struck dumb with solemn awe, and the antiwhites—so expectantly giddy at the prospect of my beat-down—seethingly brooded in silent resignation.

That same week, two things happened that allayed my remaining concerns. The first was that Riddick and Decker had fought each other in their principal's office, and both had been expelled. With all that trouble in his life, Riddick wouldn't have time for revenge. The second was when Wolf approached me in the hall. With a look of disbelief on his face, he told me he had heard a rumor that I had gone to the high school in the middle of the day and gotten in a fight. I acted surprised, and he dropped the issue. That was the first and last time anyone in the administration asked about the fight with Riddick.

In the weeks that followed, something unexpected changed at my school. It was nearly imperceptible at first, but as the days marched by it became increasingly evident. Like a smog lifting from a city never bathed by the sun, there had been an undeniable shift in the spirit of the student body.

The social obligation to pretend that antiwhitism was just and fair, which enabled antiwhites to pretentiously lecture us from an artificially constructed "moral" high ground, evaporated. Without the violence that prevented opposition to antiwhitism and examination of its tenets, the wretchedness of antiwhite assumptions, positions, and arguments conveyed its ugliness to its proponents.

Like an outdated fashion, antiwhite ideas were pushed to the fringe. The change revealed the mental sickness that compelled whites to call "good" their bane and "evil" their elixir. Some of my peers—mostly ones I didn't even know—clad themselves in Confederate flags. One artistically gifted girl even drew a flying Confederate flag across the back of her jean jacket.

The teachers and the administration continued to push their vile antiwhite screed, but the kids received it less willingly, less obediently. I wasn't alone anymore when I challenged the teachers' antiwhite lectures. Occasionally, I wasn't even the first to speak out.

The most significant personal change was how I was treated by my peers. Where once I was reviled as a heretic of antiwhitism—a "racist," an "anti-Semite," and a "hater," I had become a celebrity, an embodiment of self-sacrifice and bravery. The icing on my cake was how I was treated by the girls. I had gone from despised to desired.

To my surprise, The Triad vied for my attention—including Fox, the girl who broke my heart the previous year when she said she would never like me because of my heretical views. Now—as one of many—she wanted me. I chose one of the other members of The Triad to be my girlfriend, and I sent a simple message to Ashley Fox, *Tell her I would never like her because of her antiwhite views.*

In the span of one and a half years, I had engendered this pole-shifting transformation. But all I had done was taken a stand. All I had done was say that enough was enough. True, I suffered at the hands of the antiwhites, but I persevered. I overcame my fears. I overcame our adversaries. I had heeded the Spirit of the West, taken the fight to the enemy, and carried our banner to victory.

- Notate Bene -

On the terminology used in Crucible:

This is a true story, and my described encounters with hostile antiwhites (verbal and physical) really happened. The only change I opted to make was in updating some of the words that I used in my school years. I believe that effective language is essential to effective thought and action. In the attempt to present and empower the reader with some more effective terms that I adopted in later years in place of the more neutered vocabulary that society offered me as a child, I have incorporated more precise and powerful language like "antiwhite" into my dialogue.

Had I the white positive lexicon and dialectics that I use now, rather than the antiwhite-approved vocabulary and arguments that I used then, my victory would have empowered successive generations of white students at that school. It would have survived despite my graduation. I would have easily exposed the naked jealousy and aggression of the antiwhites from an unassailable moral high ground. My arguments would have been far more persuasive and my struggles far less severe. And I suspect, I would have converted or silenced many of the adults.

For more information on the nature of antiwhite vocabulary and thought processes, and for effective counters and alternatives to them, read my instructional book *Go Free*.

Appendix

On the words antiwhite and antiwhitism/antiwhiteism:

I became frustrated in the early '90s with the verbiage and methods used by my elders and peers in their efforts to protect the wellbeing of white people.

On one end of the spectrum, there were academics who demanded that I carefully and precisely differentiate between every category of what I would later term antiwhite and antiwhitism. They demanded that I give the antiwhites the names of their taking because to use language unsanctioned by antiwhite professors was "uncultured and ill-educated." On the other end of the spectrum, the nonacademics demanded that I give the antiwhites the insulting versions of the names of their taking, such as "commie" and "femi-Nazi".

Both approaches were spectacular failures. I experimented with various methods by which I could bring white men and women to an understanding of everything they needed to know to inspire and motivate them to protect our wellbeing.

I discovered that one of the biggest obstacles to our wellbeing was the antiwhite concept "racism," which you can read more about in *Go Free*. I studied the failures of others who attempted to address this concept, and after pondering the issue, my conclusion was that only a new, beneficial concept could defeat this harmful concept. Such a concept would have to be countervailing. It would have to be easy to teach so that, once taught, the student could quickly become the teacher to other students. It would have to undermine all of the antiwhite propaganda that we received from the news and entertainment media, academia, church, and government.

Notate Bene

I reasoned that what was needed was a concept that could turn the strength of our victimizers into our strength—that could turn the force of their billions of dollars, and control of news, entertainment and universities to *our* favor.

And the most important function that this new, beneficial concept had to serve was to create *a people* out of our deracinated race—to empower our people with the knowledge that our individual wellbeing is intrinsically linked to our group's wellbeing.

It also had to address the perceptual problem of manifold victimizers. When I would enumerate a dozen or more different antiwhite groups, two things would happen: My audience would doubt whether or not we were right in our positions (How could we be right if there were so many different groups who thought we were wrong?), and the second thing that would happen was that my audience would become afraid and apathetic (If there are so many against us, there's nothing to do but capitulate.). The concept had to resolve all of these issues and more, such as lend itself to variable intensity when used i.e. softer when persuading and more aggressive when condemning.

The great challenge was that the paradigm for discussing our wellbeing had to change. When our erstwhile leaders (those with good intentions as well as the misguided and secretly malicious) addressed our wellbeing, they cast their focus on other peoples and ideologies, dividing these threats into manifold categories, adopting the names the antiwhites gave the threats, detailing the means by which each threat harmed abstractions such as society, law and order, the church, the

Appendix

nation state, womanhood, manhood, the family (of all races). They debated the origins and potential outcomes of the threats.

Their focus was entirely in the wrong place and they couldn't see it. For them, the threat was a thing that *lived* and *breathed* and *acted*. If it could be understood, its proponents identified, its scope measured, its crimes detailed, and if this knowledge could be shared with the world, the threat would be defeated. And almost as an afterthought—we would be better off.

We needed a paradigmatic change, a new focus that centered our thinking on us, and with a new concept I hoped to engender this perceptual shift.

I briefly considered coining a new word. I looked into combining existing English and foreign words to serve this purpose. But after several attempts, I had to accept that I simply did not have the influence to propagate a new word. It seemed I was stuck with having to use a word that already existed. I looked in my dictionaries, and in the dictionaries at the city library. I questioned those who worked to protect the wellbeing of our people. I scoured materials related to our wellbeing. I found nothing.

I thought about adopting a concept that was *similar* to my desired use, but again, I faced the problem of redefining something that already existed. At last, I concluded that the word, though not in the dictionary, would have to be something that our people would instantly understand *as though it were* in the dictionary, and simultaneously satisfy all the requirements I spoke about above.

Notate Bene

Then one day the word just came to me. I had been speaking about how all of these different groups have one thing in common—they victimize our people and Western civilization. The subtle differences this way or that among these groups are irrelevant. We are white, and those who victimize us are *antiwhite*.

I was convinced the word antiwhite had to exist, but it was not in my dictionary. I looked for it in the dictionaries at the city library, but it was not there either. I was dismayed. I had relished the thought of citing a dictionary to overcome objections. But I resolved to move forward with the intuitive word despite its absence in the dictionary.

The very next opportunity I had to speak with a white man about the victimization of our people, I used antiwhite, and his eyes grew as big as dinner plates: There was a name for the people—all of them—who were victimizing us. Shortly thereafter, I added *ism* to the end of antiwhite to create *antiwhitism*, thereby naming the superset of antiwhite ideology in which there were many subsets, succinctly encompassing the varieties of Marxism, the numerous waves of feminism, and all possible nuances in academic distinction between ideologies that caused harm to my people.

Decades later, a brother in the cause for White Wellbeing discovered both "antiwhite" and "antiwhitism" in a 50-year-old dictionary, and since then in several other dictionaries. Not only do antiwhites create words to victimize us, but they delete them as well: As we think in words, if you do not have the words to speak in your own defense, you cannot think in your own defense.

Appendix

After decades of our relentless efforts to propagate essential defensive concepts like "antiwhite," they are finally breaking past the gatekeepers of the mainstream, propelled on their way by increasingly influential and powerful people, including recently the holder of the highest office in the world: President Donald J. Trump.

The power of "antiwhite" and "antiwhitism" cannot be overstated, they grant us the ability to speak and *think* effectively in our own defense. However, never combine these words with concepts that harm our people, such as the antiwhite slur "racism." To do so is to weaken "antiwhite" and strengthen "racism"—an antiwhite concept that is used to invalidate and cast as immoral everything that serves the wellbeing of white people. Therefore, never say "antiwhite racism." Just say "antiwhite." Never say "racist antiwhite propaganda." Just say "antiwhite propaganda."

On Martin Luther King Jr.:

There are a range of virtues and virtuous objectives that are ascribed to MLK, but in my childhood, his beliefs and objectives were always cited and represented by antiwhites in authority as the immaculate pinnacle of societal perfection, a quasi-religious endeavor by which society was "morally obligated" to take steps that always victimized my people. If you object to the characterization of MLK in this true story, focus your anger on those who deserve it—the antiwhites.

Notate Bene

On the words Mestizo and Mexican:

The words Mestizo and Mexican are used in this text to reference Central and South American nonwhites. White Central and South Americans as well as whites from Spain are not included in this use.

Words from the book's graphic artist (Groundhog Fury) on the censorship of his artwork:

There are two illustrations in this book that do not appear on the pages as they were originally drawn. A censor has come between you and me, presuming to know better than us what I should not draw and what drawings you should not see. May we meet again at a better time, without such interference. In the meantime, the drawings in their original form will reside in your imagination (which I trust will be able to fill the gaps), as well as on hard drives and servers you might discover. As is the case with most illustrations, your imagination did it better in the first place, anyway. :)

On the antiwhite response to this book:

Let's be real—we all know that if antiwhites conclude that my work inhibits their efforts enough to warrant misrepresenting me, they will lie about every single event and person in this book. And if one or more antiwhite oligarchs come to the same conclusion, they will fabricate "evidence" with all the resources and people that money can buy. Let their actions be a proof to you that Going Free and White

Appendix

Wellbeing are the cure to antiwhitism. And let that realization motivate you to your fullest potential to be a hero for our people.

GO FREE

A Guide to Aligning with
the Archetype of Westernkind

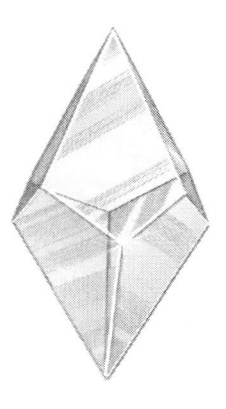

Over the course of his life, author, adventurer, entrepreneur, and White Wellbeing advocate, Jason Köhne, aka No White Guilt, has changed the lives of many with a formula he developed, refined, and has now codified in *Go Free, A Guide to Aligning with the Archetype of Westernkind*.

This formula will teach you to identify and neutralize harmful antiwhite ideas in yourself and your environment. Following this formula will enable you to access your true physical, mental, and spiritual potential as a Westman—the innate potential of our people, stifled in an age of antiwhitism.

Appendix

Simply "waking up" (or getting so-called "red pilled") to various falsehoods in the dogma of modernity is not enough. These moments of realization are essential to the healing process, but they are largely superficial. You remain infected with subconsciously-driven meme-pathogens (MPs) that undermine your well-being and potential.

With effort, you can Go Free of MPs. You can be better than you are. You can have purpose, safety, and happiness. You can access the Western Spirit within you, a power that has revolutionized the world with scientific discovery, conquered disease, charted the unknown, and triumphed in battle.

Since its public debut, Go Free (along with Köhne's live Internet broadcast "Going Free") has rescued white men and women from many self-destructive behaviors, including drug and alcohol abuse, and even suicide. Others are climbing higher than they ever imagined, and some couples have given birth, secure in the knowledge that Go Free will inoculate their children against destructive antiwhite infections, such as white-guilt.

Remain trapped in the thought diseases that cripple you, or make the life-liberating decision to Go Free!

Printed in Great Britain
by Amazon